12/92

ETHICS
A Short Introduction

About $13.35

ETHICS
A Short Introduction

Robert C. Solomon

Quincy Lee Centennial Professor of Philosophy
University of Texas–Austin

WCB Brown & Benchmark

Book Team

Developmental Editor *Deborah Reinbold*
Production Coordinator *Carla D. Arnold*

 Brown &
Benchmark
A Division of Wm. C. Brown Communications, Inc.

Vice President and General Manager *Thomas E. Doran*
Executive Managing Editor *Ed Bartell*
Executive Editor *Edgar J. Laube*
Director of Marketing *Kathy Law Laube*
National Sales Manager *Eric Ziegler*
Marketing Manager *Kathleen Nietzke*
Advertising Manager *Jodi Rymer*
Managing Editor, Production *Colleen A. Yonda*
Manager of Visuals and Design *Faye M. Shilling*

Production Editorial Manager *Vickie Putman Caughron*
Publishing Services Manager *Karen J. Slaght*
Permissions/Records Manager *Connie Allendorf*

 Wm. C. Brown Communications, Inc.

Chairman Emeritus *Wm. C. Brown*
Chairman and Chief Executive Officer *Mark C. Falb*
President and Chief Operating Officer *G. Franklin Lewis*
Corporate Vice President, Operations *Beverly Kolz*
Corporate Vice President, President of WCB Manufacturing *Roger Meyer*

Cover design and interior design by Morris Lundin

Copy editor *Martha Morss*

Library of Congress Catalog Card Number: 91–77258

ISBN 0–697–16369–5

Printed in the United States of America by Wm. C. Brown Communications, Inc.,
2460 Kerper Boulevard, Dubuque, IA 52001

10 9 8 7 6 5 4 3 2 1

For three who made the Eighties' end,
Tom Robbins, Neil Young, Kathleen Higgins

Contents

THREE
Living Well: The Virtues and the Good Life **95**

Preface

This book provides a very short but reasonably comprehensive introduction to ethics. Questions about values and contemporary American morality have been much in the news in recent years, and the demand for education in ethics has been loud and clear. What is not so clear, however, is what should be taught under this title. Ethics is one of those subjects that is both so familiar and so controversial that even its definition is a matter of considerable dispute. Does ethics require an absolute set of global commandments that apply to everyone everywhere at all times? Or is a society's ethics no more than its established customs and rules, its particular do's and don'ts? Is there room for legitimate disagreement about the most basic ethical principles? What are these principles? What is the difference between ethics and what we call morality? Is morality primarily concern for other people or is it first of all obeying the rules? Is being moral a way of acting (doing the right thing) or is it, rather, a way of thinking and feeling? Is it behavior alone that counts or must we also be concerned with the intentions and motives from which action springs?

In what follows I develop a brief account of the various views and theories that have ruled much of philosophical thinking for the past two and a half thousand years or so. While I have included an account of some of the theories of the most influential philosophers, I have emphasized the patterns of controversy and concern rather than the details of those theories or the facts about the philosophers themselves. (A very brief set of biographies can be found at the end of part 1.) I have tried to be fair in my presentation, but in my effort to keep this book readable and easily digestible by beginning students I have simplified the considerable subtlety of a great many ongoing disputes to create more memorable summaries and outlines. I have not attempted to avoid controversy, which is, after all, the very heart of the subject. In particular, I have expressed some reservations about the entire modern tradition in moral philosophy, in a short account of Nietzsche's attack on morality, for example, and by taking much more seriously than usual the often-under-fire thesis of relativism, the claim that what is morally right in one society may not be morally right in another. Chapter 3 provides more than the usual space for the rather new (but in fact very old) philosophy of virtue ethics. Virtue ethics is an ethical viewpoint that emphasizes personal character rather than abstract moral principles and consequences. I believe that the virtue ethics approach and other traditional approaches to ethics are complementary rather than contradictory, but I would argue that the traditional overemphasis on rules and results has seriously misrepresented the nature of our ordinary moral judgments. The omission of a discussion of the virtues and a general account of the good life has too often tended to render moral philosophy irrelevant to the everyday concerns. In deliberating our own actions and judging others, we do in fact pay a great deal of attention to what kind of a person one is or wants to be. I have therefore given virtue ethics a prominent place in my account here.

The issues of ethics are the issues of life in human society. We do not just behave according to instinct or impulse, and we do not live alone. We acquire goals, and we are taught ideals. We conform to patterns of acceptable social behavior and share in the praise for certain actions (generosity and bravery, for example) and the condemnation of others (utter selfishness and cowardice, for instance). We obey the law but occasionally disagree with some particular law on the basis of some higher principle. We accept these principles in turn for reasons that we may agree or disagree about. And however personal and individual we consider our values to be, we agree in our acceptance of certain very general assumptions, for example, the necessity of self-respect, the right to live a decent life, the importance of love and friendship in our lives, and the importance of doing the right thing—though we may not always agree on just what that is. It would be a mistake, however, to think of the variety of theories and concerns in ethics as a grab bag or smorgasbord from which each student can pick and choose according to personal taste. Indeed, if there is one compelling belief that has motivated philosophers since Plato, it is the idea that there is a correct theory of ethics: that the goals, ideals, rules, and principles governing behavior do form a coherent and comprehensible system, which it is the purpose of the study of ethics to understand.

On the other hand, people often have conflicts of interest and disagreements about what is the right thing to do. The history of ethics shows us how philosophers disagree about ethical theories. Nevertheless, the reason why we disagree, both in particular cases and in the most general philosophical debates, is that each of us believes that we are objectively right. Ethics, unlike one's favorite flavor of ice cream, is not just a matter of taste. Our actions and our moral judgments can be challenged, and we are expected to give reasons to back them up. When we disagree in ethics, our differences of opinion can become bitter, even violent. Accordingly, it is necessary to understand the views we disagree with and come to grips with the nature of our disagreements. But understanding the other side does not mean giving up one's own convictions. Appreciating the variety of ethical theories does not mean that it's all a matter of opinion.

The aim of the study of ethics and the aim of this book is to help the student think about ethical issues, from the most concrete personal problems ("I promised my highschool sweetheart that I wouldn't go out with anyone else while I'm away at college, but then I met . . .") to various puzzles and paradoxes ("Why would a person act against his or her own best interests?" "What's wrong with blackmail if it's an exercise of freedom of speech?") to the most general ethical questions ("What is happiness?" "How does one resolve a conflict of fundamental principles?"). Ethical theories have been formulated to help us think about right conduct in the concrete situations of life, to organize the enormous number of opinions, feelings, and intuitions we have about what is right and what is wrong. At the same time, particular personal problems often arise just because of our awareness of the broader ethical questions. What seems like an innocent action may nevertheless set a disturbing precedent. A course of action might further one's personal ambitions, but only by breaking some basic moral rule (for example, the prohibition against lying) or violating one's sense of personal integrity. Our awareness of the consequences and the significance of our actions adds a dimension to our thinking. A student may know that he or she will have a better chance of getting a job with a small fabrication on the résumé; but even if no one will ever find out, what does it mean to have lied? A person may want out of a tedious marriage because happiness seems to lie elsewhere. But what does it mean to abandon a marriage, and what will happen to the others involved? Ethics involves the unity of concrete human concerns and a more general awareness and appreciation of worthy goals, ideals, rules, and principles. To adapt a phrase from one of the great moral philosophers, Immanuel Kant, we might say that ethics without reference to particular actions and feelings is empty, but action and feeling devoid of ethics are blind.

One of the central themes of this book is the insistence that ethics is a shared effort. My debts to friends, colleagues, and students are in evidence on every one of the following pages. (I will refrain from blaming them for any mistakes.) Some of the orientation of this book has been influenced by the new revisions in classical ethics promoted by Alasdair MacIntyre, William Gass, Frithjof Bergmann, Edmund Pincoffs, Bernard

Williams, Martha Nussbaum, Richard Taylor, Michael Stocker, Michael Slote, and others. The classical substance of the book I digested under the tutelage of Betty Flowers, Charles Stevenson, William Frankena, Julius Moravsik, and Stuart Hampshire. I owe a very special debt of gratitude to Lee Bowie and Meredith Michaels, Paul Woodruff, Kathleen Higgins, Shirley Hull, Elaine Engelhardt, and Janet Sepasi for her insightful reading and her fabulous teaching assistance. Several friends and colleagues in the publishing world helped give birth to the book, beginning with Kaye Pace of McGraw-Hill who helped me develop and publish an earlier version entitled *Ethics: A Brief Introduction*, Cynthia Ward who guided me in preparation of what began as a second edition of that book but soon turned into a new and quite different project, and Meredith Morgan of Brown and Benchmark who happily convinced me to publish the final result with them. My thanks as well to the dozen or so readers who have reviewed and rigorously criticized the various drafts of both books and to the many students who have been my audience for so many years.

Robert C. Solomon
Austin, TX

PART ONE

Introduction to Ethics

Last Thursday, you went out for lunch with an acquaintance from biology class, a nice-enough fellow but not someone you consider a candidate for lifelong friendship. As you were wolfing down your last bite of cheeseburger, you suddenly gulped and flushed; you realized that you had forgotten your wallet. You were flat broke. Embarrassed, you entreated your classmate to lend you five dollars, which you would, of course, pay back on Tuesday. Today is Wednesday; you forgot.

Now you are doubly embarrassed, for having had to borrow the money in the first place and then for having forgotten to pay it back when promised. You are tempted, momentarily, to ignore the entire awkward situation, just to assume—what may well be true—that your classmate has forgotten about the loan. (After all, it is only five dollars.) But maybe he hasn't forgotten, or, at least, he'll remember it when he sees you. For an irrational instant, you consider dropping the class, but then you realize that would be ridiculous. It seems highly unlikely, since it would be very embarrassing for him, that he would actually ask you for the money. Any way, you aren't close friends and don't generally talk to each other. So what's the difference? You make up your mind not to repay the debt.

But now, small hints of large doubts start interrupting your day. You are convinced that no harm will come to you. The fellow knows none of your friends, and it is hardly likely that he will announce to the class or the world that you are a deadbeat. And yet, it's ruining your day, and it may well ruin other days. "If only I could get rid of this guilty feeling," you say to yourself. But it is not just a feeling; it is a new and wholly unwelcome sense of who you are. A voice inside of you (sometimes it sounds like your own voice; occasionally it seems to be your mother's) keeps whispering, "Deadbeat, deadbeat" (and worse). Already distracted from your work, you start speculating, "What if we all were to forget about our debts?" Your first response is that you would probably be washing dishes at the Burger Shoppe, since no one would ever lend anyone money. Your second response is that everyone doesn't forget, but this argument doesn't make you feel any better. It reminds you that in a world where most people pay their debts, you are one of the scoundrels who does not. You start rationalizing: "After all, I need the money more than he does." In a final moment of belligerence, you smash your fist on the table and say, within hearing distance of the people sharing your library table, "The only person I have to worry about is me!"

There is an embarrassed silence. Then you walk over to the bank of phones. You dial: "Hello, Harris? Remember that five dollars you loaned me?"

The point of this little scenario is to capture the day-to-day nature of ethics. Even such a simple situation involves conflicting interests, profound moral principles, and the nagging voice of conscience, culminating in a quiet but nevertheless telling conclusion concerning the sort of person you are. This case does not involve any of the more notoriously difficult social problems or life-or-death decisions so vehemently debated today, such as the abortion issue, the legitimacy of war, the plight of the homeless in a land of affluence, or starving children in a world awash with surplus food. But, ultimately, the considerations that enter into our debates on these global issues reflect our habits and opinions in the most ordinary circumstances. Our politics express who we are and what we believe, and even our most abstract ideologies reveal (although often in a convoluted and even reactionary way) the principles and prejudices of everyday life.

What is Ethics?

Ethics is that part of philosophy that is concerned with living well, being a good person, doing the right thing, getting along with other people, and wanting the right things in life. Ethics is essential to living in society, any society, with its various traditions, practices, and institutions. Of course, those traditions, practices, and institutions can and must themselves be assessed according to ethical standards, but they themselves determine many of the rules and expectations that define the ethical outlook of the people living within them. Ethics therefore has both a social and a personal dimension, but it is not at all easy, in theory or in practice, to separate these. Moral judgment is both the product of society and one of its constitutive features. What we call our personal values are for the most part learned together and shared by a great many people. Indeed, those values we consider most personal are typically not those that are most idiosyncratic but rather those that are most common, and most profound—respect for human (and animal) life, outrage at being the victim of a lie, compassion for those much worse off than yourself, and an insistence on personal integrity in the face of adversity.

The word *ethics* refers both to a discipline—the study of our values and their justification—and to the subject matter of that discipline—the actual values and rules of conduct by which we live. The two meanings merge in the fact that we behave (and misbehave) according to a complex and continually changing set of rules, customs, and expectations; consequently, we are forced to reflect on our conduct and attitudes, to justify and sometimes to revise them.

Why do we need to study ethics as a discipline? Isn't it enough that we have ethics, that we do (most of us, most of the time) act according to our values and rules? But part of our ethics is understanding ethics, that is, acting for reasons and being able to defend our actions if called upon to do so. It is not enough, after the age of eight or so, simply to do what you are told; it is just as important to know the reason why, and to be able to say no when you think an act is wrong. So, too, it is not enough to have strong political opinions on this or that controversial social issue. It is important to have reasons, to have a larger vision, to have a framework within which to house and defend your opinions. The study of ethics teaches us to appreciate the overall system of reasons within which having ethics makes sense. Understanding what we are doing and why is just as essential to ethics as doing the right thing.

We learn ethics, typically, a piece at a time. Our education begins in childhood, first and foremost, with examples, continuous demonstrations of "normal" behavior. We watch our parents and our older siblings, before we know what they are doing, and we imitate them, no doubt before we know what *we* are doing. Our education continues with a number of instructions and prohibitions, such as "Don't hit your little sister" and "You should share your toys with your friends." The recognition of authority is essential, of course, beginning with "You do what your father says" and culminating in "because it's the law, that's why." But it is also learning reasons, such as "because if everyone did that, there wouldn't be any left" or "because it will make her unhappy." Ultimately, we learn the specialized language of morality and the more abstract reasons for doing or refraining from certain actions, such as "because it is your duty" and "because it is immoral." By this time we have begun to learn that ethics is not just a varied collection of do's and don'ts but a system of values and principles which tie together in a reasonable and coherent way to make our society and our lives as civilized and as happy as possible. The study of ethics is the final step in this process of education—the understanding of that system as such and the way that all our particular values and principles fit into it.

Change, Choice, and Pluralism

Our understanding of ethics is complicated enormously by the fact that, as a living system, our ethics is continually changing. Consider, for example, the tremendous changes that our society has experienced over just the past few decades in the realm of sexual morality; today, we accept behavior which would have been wanton immorality sixty years ago (for example, topless beachwear for men). Similar changes have taken place in our concept of personal roles and career options. Only twenty years ago, many people considered it unethical for a wife to work except in cases of dire family need, but it was perfectly acceptable—in fact, even commendable—for a husband to spend so much time working at his career that he virtually never saw his children or did anything but work. Today, many people do not find such behavior praiseworthy but, rather, akin to a disease (workaholism). Attitudes toward authority have also changed dramatically. Fifty years ago, the attitude of most young men, when drafted into the army (or invited to enlist) was unquestioning acceptance. Twenty-five years ago, those who refused to be drafted and otherwise resisted authority were praised by many people as moral heroes. What this means, and whether there are underlying values that support both obedience and disobedience, depending on the circumstances, are some of the most important questions of ethics.

We live in a society filled with change and disagreement, in which each generation tends to reexamine the values and actions of the older generation, in which doing what you are told or simply conforming to tradition is not necessarily a mark of moral goodness but may be considered cowardice or evidence of a lack of character. Our ethics, in other words, involves choice. In fact, having and permitting individual freedom of choice is itself one of the most noteworthy values of our ethics. To choose between alternative courses of action or opposed values requires intelligent deliberation and some sense of the reasons why we should choose one rather than another. Each of us must select a way of life, perhaps a career or a profession, perhaps a life of creativity or adventure. We might follow in our parents' footsteps or we might go off on a completely different path. But we must choose. Each of us must decide whether or not to get married, and when and to whom. We must decide whether or not to have children, how many, and how they will be raised; such decisions affect the lives of others in the most direct and dramatic sense possible. Every day, each of us decides whether or not to engage in a dozen small misdeeds and occasionally, whether to commit a misdemeanor, such as driving on a deserted highway at 80 miles per hour or taking a box of paperclips home from the office.

The importance of choice in ethics is often confused with the notion that we choose our values, or that values are merely subjective and that everyone has his or her own personal values. This assumption is misleading. Most of ethics involves decisions between already-established possibilities and already-available reasons. A student deciding between joining the Navy or going to law school does indeed have an important choice to make, but the alternatives and their values are provided by the society as a whole. (There must already be a military to join or a role for lawyers in society.) One does not choose the alternatives; one chooses among the alternatives. And once the choice is made, he or she is suddenly situated in a world of "objective" values—the iron-clad rules of the military or the stringent standards of the legal profession. In ethics we face choices, but the personal values we thereby endorse are virtually never one's own values alone. The very nature of values is such that they must be shared; they exist over and above those who embrace them.

Nevertheless, there is a sense, defended by the twentieth-century French existentialist Jean-Paul Sartre, in which we do choose our values, and ourselves, every time we make an ethical decision. By deciding not to take advantage of a loophole in the tax laws, for example, one personally affirms the priority of compliance over individual gain. By acting in one way rather than another, we support one value rather than another, one sense of who we are rather than another. For Sartre ethics is largely a matter of individual choice and commitment rather than of obedience to already-established authorities.

We live in an ethically *pluralist* society. This means that there is no single code of ethics but several different sets of values and rules in a variety of contexts, communities, and subcultures. Professional and business people in our society emphasize individual success and mobility; some cultural communities stress the importance of group identity and stable ethnic traditions. Some college and urban communities are notably more liberal in their tolerance for eccentricity and deviance than the more conservative suburban neighborhoods surrounding them. Even what would seem to be the most basic rules of morality vary from culture to culture, neighborhood to neighborhood, context to context. Thus, we find our Supreme Court, the ultimate arbiter of laws if not morals, insisting on "community standards" as the test for what is permissible, in the case of pornography, for instance.

Many people in our society insist that the ultimate value is individual freedom. But personal freedom has its costs, among them the possible inconvenience and deprivation of others. One person's freedom may well be an infringement of another person's rights, and many people thus argue there are issues of morality and justice that are more important than individual freedom. Such conflicts in ethics are not easily reconciled; in fact, they may be irreconcilable. But that makes it all the more important that we understand the nature of the conflicts and at least know how to try to reconcile our differences instead of intransigently shouting our views at one another, imposing them on others, or simply storming out of the room. Being reasonable in such situations is much of what ethical discussion and debate are about, and pluralism provides much of the motive. If one isn't clear about the nature and justification of one's own values, he or she won't be in a position to understand the nature and justification of other people's values. And if one doesn't understand other people's values, neither will one understand how they conflict or might be brought into harmony with one's own.

Ethics and Ethos

The word *ethics* comes from the Greek word *ethos,* meaning "character" or "custom," and the derivative phrase *ta ethika,* which the philosophers Plato and Aristotle used to describe their own studies of Greek values and ideals. Accordingly, ethics is first of all a concern for character, including what we blandly call being a good person, but it is also a concern for the overall character of an entire society, which is called its *ethos.* Ethics is participation in, and an understanding of, an ethos; it is the effort to understand the social rules that govern and limit our behavior, especially those fundamental rules, such as prohibitions against killing and stealing, the commandments that one should honor thy parents, and respect for the rights of others, which we call *morality.*

The close connection between ethics and social customs, or *mores,* which shares its etymological root with the word *morality,* inevitably raises the question of whether morality is nothing but the customs of our particular society, our ethics nothing but the rules of our particular ethos. On the one hand, ethics and morality are very closely tied to the laws and the customs of a particular society. Kissing in public and making an enormous profit in a business transaction are considered immoral in some societies, not in others. On the other hand, some laws or customs endorsed by an entire society have more importance than others.

The rules of etiquette may be merely a matter of local custom or taste, but the prohibition against cannibalism, for example, seems to have much more universal power and justification than the simple reminder, "That just isn't done around here."

One way of circumscribing the principles of morality—as distinguished from rules of etiquette and standards of good taste, for example—is to insist that these are not the province of only a particular society or subculture within society but, rather, rules which we apply to all people everywhere and expect them to obey. We might be happy to accept, and even be charmed by, the fact that people in another culture eat food with wooden sticks instead of forks or enjoy music based on quarter tones without a discernible melody. But when we consider the culture of gangland America, for example, or the satanic rituals of certain cults, our tolerance diminishes and we find ourselves quite willing to impose our own values and standards. Ethics provides the basic rules of an ethos, but those rules are not limited to that ethos. Ethics needs a culture in which to be cultivated, but that does not mean that ethics consists of just the rules of that particular culture. Morality, according to many philosophers, is that set of rules which applies to all cultures, whatever their customs or traditions.

An ethos is that core of attitudes, beliefs, and feelings that gives coherence and vitality to a people (in ancient Greek, an *ethnos,* a word significantly similar to *ethos*). It may be spelled out explicitly in terms of laws, but much of an ethos resides in the hearts and minds of the people, in what they expect of one another and what they expect of themselves, in what they like and dislike, in what they value and disdain, hope and fear. An essential part of our ethos, for example, is that individual success, or "standing out in the crowd," is desirable. There is no law or moral principle that commands that this should be so, but our ethics very much depends upon the values of individualism and achievement. In some societies, by way of contrast, individual ambitions and eccentricities are unacceptable. "The nail that sticks out is the one that gets hammered down,'' reads a traditional Japanese proverb. We should not assume that all *ethè* (the plural of *ethos*) are the same, even in their most basic values and visions.

Morality

Ethics includes the whole range of acceptable social and personal practices, from the rules of common courtesy to the institutions that determine the kinds of work we do, the kinds of friends we have, and the ways we relate to both family and strangers. Morality, on the other hand, is something more specific, a subset of ethical rules that are of particular importance and transcend the boundaries of any particular ethos or situation. Thus, we believe, it is always immoral to be cruel to children, even if doing so is a repetitive pattern of family life. Morality, accordingly, is thought to be a weightier term than ethics. If someone refuses to play fair or to honor a verbal contract, we might say that he or she is unethical, but we would not say immoral. If a person abuses children or poisons his in-laws, however, we would call such behavior immoral, indicating the seriousness of these violations. Morality consists of the most basic and inviolable rules of a society.

The distinction between ethics and morality—ethics as the whole of our sense of self and our place in society and morality as the core, universal, most inviolable rules in any society—is not always followed in either ordinary conversation or philosophical theorizing. Indeed, the curious history of these terms shows how much our very conception of ethics and morality has shifted over the centuries along with the more obvious shifts in the practices they evaluate and prescribe. The current definition of the word *morality*, for example, displays a range of meanings that shows both the ancient sense in which the terms *morality* and *ethics* embrace the whole of human behavior and the very narrow nineteenth-century sense in which morality is obsessively concerned with sexual behavior. The *Random House Dictionary,* for example, lists the following as definitions of morality: (1) conformity to rules of right conduct, (2) moral quality of character, (3) virtue in sexual matters, (4) a doctrine or system of morals, (5) moral instruction. We shall see how these various conceptions play off against one another in current as well as traditional debates in ethics. But for our purposes here, we will be using *morality* to refer to conformity to rules of right conduct and to the rules themselves. But even this basic definition is not sufficient. Many rules in ethics ("Don't be rude") and even in etiquette ("Don't eat your burrito with a spoon") seem to be rules of right conduct. What distinguishes moral rules is a number of distinctive features that are emphasized (in different ways and with many mixed opinions) by philosophers and other moral theorists. Here are four of the most-often mentioned:

1. *Moral rules have great importance.*

   Moral rules, however else they may be characterized, are of indisputable importance. They are like trump cards in certain games, overpowering all other considerations. In our opening example, the obligation to repay a loan outweighed purely personal concerns, such as one's embarrassment or one's own need for money. Indeed, it is the mark of morality that the amount of money involved is not what is important. The obligation would override self-interest whether the amount involved were ten cents or a thousand dollars. It is sometimes suggested that moral rules are those without which a society could not survive or, at least, could not function in what it considers a civilized way. For example, how could there be promises or contracts at all—the basis of much of our lives—if the respect for promises and contracts were not more important than a person's personal advantage in breaking them? Furthermore, to call a person or an act immoral is to condemn that person or act in the strongest possible terms, just as to say that an issue is a moral issue is to say that it is of the utmost importance.

2. *Morality consists of universal rules.*

Morality is rule-governed in that it tells us what sorts of things to do and not to do by way of general classes and types of acts, such as "One ought to repay debts" or "Don't ever tell a lie." Morality involves obedience to such rules, but it also requires understanding, knowledge of the rules, and the recognition that they are necessary and obligatory. Furthermore, moral rules are distinguished by the fact that they are universal; they apply to everyone everywhere. They are not just local customs or the rules of some particular practice (such as staying behind the line of scrimmage in football).

3. *Moral rules are rational, disinterested and objective.*

There are special reasons for acting morally, for example, "because it is my obligation." These reasons require special concepts, such as duty, obligation, and principle, and a special kind of upbringing in which these concepts are inculcated. The ability to think in terms of abstract principles (e.g., "Never tell a lie") and reasons (e.g., "If everyone lied, no one could believe anyone") is often called *rationality.* One of the key features of rationality, according to many philosophers, is its universality. Unlike most emotions and desires, for example, reason is the same in everyone. Everyone may have his or her own ideal of love or pet peeve, but we all necessarily share the conclusions of reason (e.g., "Two plus two equals four"). Thus it is sometimes said that, if a reason is a good reason, it will be so for every rational creature, and morality has been defined by some philosophers as the rules and actions of a completely rational person. Many philosophers, however, question whether rationality is itself objective and universal, or whether what counts as practical reason in ethics might differ from culture to culture. (It also differs from philosophical theory to philosophical theory.)

It is also said that morality is rational, in part, because it is *disinterested*. A moral, rule is disinterested in that it applies without regard to one's own personal interests or feelings or status in the case and it remains oblivious to the status of the people to whom it applies. (Think of the classic image of Justice wearing a blindfold, thus being blind to the particular identities of the people who stand before her.) One has an obligation to repay a loan whether or not one needs the money, whether or not repaying the loan will advance one's interests in other ways (for example, making it easier to obtain another loan in the future) and whether or not the person who made the loan needs the money back. Of course, one can sometimes use a moral principle to one's own advantage, but the moral principle itself is formulated to no one's advantage and with no particular person's interests in mind. To so insist that morality is independent of subjective feelings and interests is to say that morality is *objective*. Thus rationality and disinterestedness imply objectivity. "Adultery is wrong!" does not mean "I don't like adultery" or "Our society disapproves of adultery." A moral rule is objective insofar as its correctness is quite distinct from what particular people, or even whole societies, happen to think of it. What's right is right and what's wrong is wrong.

4. *Morality is concerned with other people.*
Morality essentially involves consideration of interests other than one's own and is thus well summarized in the various versions of the so-called golden rule. "Do unto others as you would have them do unto you" is found in almost every ethical system. In the Hebrew Talmud, for example, it is presented as the basic principle of ethics: "What is hurtful to yourself do not to your fellow man; that is the whole of the Torah [the Jewish Scripture] and the remainder is but commentary." The Confucian *Analects* tell us, "Do not unto others what you would not they should do unto you." The Taoist *T'ai*

Shang Kan Ying Pien says, "Regard your neighbor's gain as your own gain, and regard your neighbor's loss as your own loss." The Buddha insisted, "Hurt not others with that which pains yourself." And Mohammed commanded, "Do not unto others what you would not they should do unto you." The slight differences among these versions of the rule may make a considerable difference in morals. Consider the difference, for example, between the warning that what you do to others might be done to you in turn and the appeal to compassion, that you should think about other people's feelings in the same way that you think of your own. Most of the versions refer to one's own possible pains and interests. But, at the same time, every version makes reference to the interests of other people, and this is the essence of morality; it presupposes an awareness of the interests of others as well as of one's own. The opposition between morality and mere self-interest, however, does not imply that to be moral you must always go against your own self-interest. Indeed, one of the most common arguments for morality is that it ultimately serves each person's self-interest to obey the rules of morality and pay attention to the interests and well-being of others.

The most prominent single philosopher of modern ethics, who is, more than anyone else, responsible for the emphasis on morality in ethics is Immanuel Kant. Kant was a German who wrote at the end of the eighteenth century. Kant introduces the most distinctive philosophical version of the golden rule and defends the strictest characterization of morality in the history of ethics. His somewhat technical version of the golden rule is "Act so that the maxim (principle) of your action can be willed as universal law." Kant's thesis is a formal version of the demand that morality is essentially universal and that moral principles are universalizable; moral rules always apply to everyone and never refer to just one person or that person's own interests alone. But where most conceptions of morality tend to give equal emphasis to both one's own interests and the interests of others (as in the standard formulations of the golden rule), Kant separates self-interest and morality completely. Indeed, insofar as an act is based on inclinations of any kind (whether personal desire or sympathy for the other fellow), that act is not considered "morally worthy." Morality, Kant says, is a law unto itself, "categorical" and independent of all personal interests and inclinations. Accordingly, Kant analyzes morality in terms of what he calls the "categorical imperative." An imperative, of course, is simply a command, and morality for Kant consists of rules. Using the term *categorical* is a strong way of insisting on the absolute nature of moral rules. According to Kant, morality is thoroughly objective, a product of reason ("practical reason"). A moral principle has nothing to do with personal interest or the particular circumstances of the case; it is thoroughly disinterested. It is also what Kant calls *a priori,* or "prior to" any particular cases or moral judgments we might make. In Kant's ethics the four basic features of morality are brought together into a singularly powerful conception of morality. Many philosophers and readers have challenged this conception as too narrow and impersonal, even as heartless, and many others have come to Kant's defense and suggested more flexible, less dogmatic interpretations of his ethics. But even in its most rigid expression, Kant's model of morality is so systematic and persuasive that it is impossible to study ethics without coming to grips with it. Indeed, some ethicists would say that the study of ethics today is a study of variations and objections to the theory set out by Kant some two hundred years ago. Still others would say that the heart of contemporary ethics is the rejection of this same moral theory.

Ethics, Ethos, and Morality: The Problem of Relativism

To understand the ethos and the ethics of various peoples is one of the aims of the science of anthropology. Ethics, however, is something more than this. For example, as the great French anthropologist Claude Levi-Strauss commented in a 1970 interview:

> When I witness certain decisions or modes of behavior in my own society, I am filled with indignation and disgust, whereas if I observe similar behavior in a so-called primitive society, I make no attempt at a value judgment. I try to understand it.

Philosophers often distinguish between *descriptive* statements and *prescriptive* statements; the former tell us what the facts are; the latter tell us what ought to be. It is one thing to describe what people do and what they value; it is something more to enter into their lives and tell them what they ought to do and value. In anthropology, we can and should be content with description. In ethics, however, our descriptions are always mixed with prescriptions, for we are not merely trying to understand ourselves. We are also trying to live well and do what is right to do.

Ethics is not a descriptive science but an active participation in a set of values, a way of life. But, as we have already noted, the notion of a way of life leaves open the question of whether some ways of life (e.g., human sacrifice, military aggression for the fun of it) might be morally wrong. Morality, as characterized in the preceding section, is universal and not just one set of values among others. Moral rules, accordingly, are applied not just to one's own ethos but to all others as well. When European explorers found out that the natives of the New World practiced human sacrifice, they did not simply note it as an anthropological curiosity; they were horrified (despite the fact that the Inquisition was systematically killing many people in Europe in the name of Christianity). When Northerners visited the Southern states during the years preceding the Civil War, many did not see slavery as a quaint custom or a local necessity; they viewed it as the grossest immorality and a pretext for war. When some rural German philosophers visited the sweatshops of London and Manchester at the beginning of the industrial revolution, they were indignant, and they started fomenting a social revolution. Karl Marx was one of them, and, not surprisingly, he formulated his revolutionary manifesto in the universal vocabulary of morality and justice, not just in economic terms.

Moral rules are more than mores and customs because they claim to outline the conditions which any society must fulfill and are applicable to everyone everywhere. The moral prohibition on incest, according to some influential anthropologists and biologists, is not only a universal moral rule but built right into our genes as well. (Partial evidence for this is the prevalence of incest taboos among most animal species, although such inferences from other species to human morality are always to be made with extreme caution.) The moral rule "Thou shalt not steal" seems to be not just a custom common in many societies but the necessary condition for there being any secure sense of ownership at all. The moral rule that it is wrong to lie seems to be the precondition of being able to believe what other people say. Imagine visiting a city, for example, where most of the directions you receive are lies, as the natives mischievously send you off in this direction and that. After a short time, you will refuse to listen to any directions at all, knowing the odds against their being correct. A society can exist with some lying, of course, but it is impossible to imagine a society in which most people did not tell the truth most of the time.

Moral rules are considered to be basic rules because they outline the conditions for the very existence of society. Certain moral rules may be of special importance in particular societies. For example, cheating and plagiarism are considered moral transgressions in a college community because they undermine the conditions for a truly competitive, creative community. Violating a contract and refusing to pay one's bills are considered especially serious violations in business because such acts threaten the very existence of the business community. Some moral rules seem to be of special importance in virtually every society: sexual mores and family relationships, for example, have a profound importance in almost every culture because having babies and raising them is obviously essential to the continuation of the culture.

Although morals are basic to the existence of a society, changing social and economic conditions can dramatically change morals. For instance, the morality of having children changes dramatically in times of serious overpopulation or underpopulation. If a population seems to be increasing to the breaking point, many people insist that it is immoral to have more than one or two children, even when a particular family can easily afford them. In societies eager to increase their population on the other hand, not having children is typically considered a moral failing. (In underpopulated ancient Rome, for example, pregnancy was so encouraged that there was not even a word for contraception.) Indeed, there are overpopulated societies in which even murder is taken less seriously, and the death of hundreds of people from disease and starvation is considered merely a normal part of daily life. Or, to take a more agreeable example, in a society in which there is much to be accomplished (for instance, in colonial America), work becomes a virtue, even an ethic unto itself. Just lying back and enjoying life, a virtue in some aristocratic and leisurely societies, is recast as laziness, a vice.

These variations in morals from society to society have naturally troubled moralists and ethical philosophers who would like to find a single, universal set of standards as the basis of all societies. Some ethicists avoid this problem by restricting their attention to the moral rules and the logic of moral thinking in their own society, without even attempting to pass judgment on societies other than their own. Other ethicists consider the variations within a set of moral rule to discern an underlying universal rule. Consider, for example, the various senses of *stealing*.

Aristotle and much of medieval society considered the taking of profits in business transactions a mode of stealing, and Marxist societies regard the very institution of private property as a form of theft. ("Property is theft," wrote a nineteenth-century French socialist named Proudhon, who was quoted by Marx.) On Wall Street, it is just another day's business to take an entire company away from its unwilling owners, in an unfriendly acquisition, so long as the buyer is willing to pay for 51 percent of the stock and an expensive team of lawyers and strategists. What counts as stealing is often determined by context. In baseball, running unexpectedly from one canvas sack to another is called stealing a base, but this is a legitimate part of the game. (Stealing a base by actually picking up one of those sacks and running off the field with it, however, is not part of the game and thus illegitimate.) In the face of very different views of what might be called stealing, it would not seem easy to isolate some underlying if very complicated universal principle, summarized simply and without qualification as "Thou shalt not steal," that applies to medieval life and Marxism as well as Wall Street and baseball. But one could argue, for instance, that all of these variations are but special instances of the general rule, "Do not take that to which you are not entitled." Of course, one would then, in any particular application of the rule, have to specify what warrants entitlement. Aristotle accepted the idea of private property and the desirability of wealth but rejected the legitimacy of exchange for profit. Marx rejected the institution of private ownership and so saw all accumulation of wealth as theft. Stealing a base is a legitimate play in baseball but disrupting the field by taking the sack is not. So although what counts as stealing may vary from context to context, the underlying moral prohibition remains the same.

There are ethicists, however, called *relativists,* who reject this idea that there are universal moral principles, with or without local variations and contextual qualifications. Relativists argue that morality is relative to an ethos and limited to that ethos. "What is moral in India can get a man hanged in France," wrote one eighteenth-century relativist, his conclusion being that morals are nothing but the local customs of a particular community. This conclusion might not upset us if it meant only that certain customs and mores—eating habits and attitudes toward pets, for example—were different in different societies. Nor would it be especially troublesome if it were only a way of reminding us that particular moral rules and actions differ from place to place—whether charging high interest rates counts as stealing or whether early abortion counts as murder. What is upsetting is the idea that cold-blooded murder or slavery might be moral in a certain setting, in feudal Japan or ancient Greece, for example, and that we have no right whatever to condemn them.

Relativism in its extreme form claims that differences among societies are much more than superficial. It insists that the most basic rules of morality are different too, that not only what counts as murder, for example, but even murder itself has different moral status in different societies. For example, in some ancient cultures, religious sacrifices, such as the Greek Agamemnon's slaughter of his daughter and the Aztec annual vivisectionist rituals, were considered legitimate forms of killing. Trying to bridge the cross-cultural gap, one might say that such cases are not murder because there was some reason for the killing, namely, a religious reason. But this limp suggestion would eliminate as murder virtually all cases of killing except involuntary manslaughter (which is not murder) and the very rare cases of intentional murder without any (conscious) reason at all. One might make the purely verbal point that murder by definition means "wrongful killing," and thus all murder is (necessarily) wrong, but this just moves the question back one step to killing, and whether killing is always considered wrong. Relativism continues to be one of the most pressing problems in ethics, and it will follow us like a shadow through many of the discussions in this book. A society's ethos is partially determined by its morals, but does the ethos alone define morals? Is morality, like etiquette and entertainment, just the product of a particular society, or does it underlie the ethè of all societies as their basic foundation? Are we justified in extending our moral principles to people across the world? Or is this, too, just another example of imperialism, the unwanted imposition of one culture's tastes and standards upon another which itself is considered, by many people, to be morally wrong?

Egoism and Altruism

Just as some philosophers have been suspicious that what we call morality may be only the projection of our own ethics onto other people, many philosophers and a great many other people, such as most economists, have suspected (or presumed) that what moves people to act is virtually never morality or the interests of other people (except, perhaps, their closest kin) but rather their own interests, which may or may not coincide with the moral rules. Of course, such behavior in one's own interest need not be crude or inconsiderate, and it need not even serve one's own interests in the short run. Indeed, the mark of smart or enlightened self-interest, or what we call *prudence,* is precisely the wisdom to be considerate and concerned with the well-being of others if only as a means to furthering one's own long term interests. Prudence is still self-interest, but it involves caution, social awareness, and long-term thinking. It may be an enormous thrill to drive your car at top speeds down a winding country road, but you could easily be killed or, given the occasional pedestrian loitering in the middle of the road, kill someone. It may be what you want at the moment, but it is not prudent. It may seem to be in your self-interest to cheat on an exam when that one extra grade will get you on the Dean's list. But you may be caught and expelled, you may be initiating a habit that will ruin or deprive your educational talents later on, you will deprive yourself of the opportunity to prove your worth on your own, and you will probably lower yourself in your own eyes and in the eyes of any other students who see you. Cheating may be in your immediate self-interest but it is not at all prudent. Thus prudence, unlike crude, thoughtless self-interest, is often in conformity with the dictates of morality. But is morality motivated by nothing more than prudence, or is prudence, as enlightened self-interest, still something short of truly moral behavior?

One of the most enduring debates in ethics (dating back to Plato, at least) concerns this question of motivation in morals. Do we, in fact, always act for the sake of our self-interest? Or do we, at least sometimes, act for the sake of duty and duty alone, or for the sake of others without regard to our own self-interest? Traditionally, this dichotomy between acting out of one's own self-interest and acting for the benefit of others has been marked by the terms egoism and altruism. *Egoism* is acting out of self-interest. *Altruism* is acting for the benefit of others. Altruism may be based on some sense of attachment or compassion, but it need not be. One could be altruistic on principle, always taking other people's interests as more important that his own. Like many ethical categories, egoism and altruism are used to refer to the consequences as well as the motivation of behavior. Egoism is action that benefits oneself. Altruism is action that benefits others. But the primary meaning of these terms is and must be tied to motivation, not consequences. One can, perhaps despite one's bad intentions, benefit others, but such behavior is not by any means altruistic. One often does, unfortunately, fail in one's efforts to help others, occasionally benefiting oneself in the process. This does not make one's behavior self-interested.

On the one hand, egoism is obviously antithetical to morality; it emphasizes concern for one's own interests whatever the rules and whatever one's obligations. One can, however, be moral and fulfill one's obligations just as a means to satisfying one's interests. Should this count as moral behavior? On the other hand, egoism, many ethicists have argued, is the sole basis for any human behavior, moral or otherwise. If this is true, however, how is it possible ever to act for the sake of morality, unless our obligations also satisfy our interests? Are we moral (when we are moral) only because being so is in our interests? If I give money to a beggar and feel good that I have done so, have I in fact given him the money only in order to feel good afterward? Such questions raise the age-old issue of human nature, and whether we are indeed by nature selfish creatures or, rather, social beings in whom concern for others and at least some minimal sense of compassion is equally natural. But they also raise the question of what strategies we use to get along in life. Our behavior, after all, is a product not only of what we naturally feel but also of our thinking about what we, as rational creatures, ought to do.

Philosophers accordingly distinguish between psychological egoism and ethical egoism. *Psychological egoism* is the psychological theory that everything that we do, we do for our own interests, whether or not the same act serves other people's interests or moral obligations. *Ethical egoism* is the view that one ought to act in one's own interests. Of course, if psychological egoism is true, one cannot help but act in one's own interests. Nevertheless, the two positions are distinct. One might believe that all people are motivated by their own interests and nevertheless try to make sure that these interests coincide with the common good and morality. The purpose of punishment, for example, is to offset the personal benefits of wrongdoing. And one might believe that people are not naturally out for their own interests but that they ought to be so. Imagine a person who believes, for instance, that most of the damage done in the world is caused by do-gooders who ought to mind their own business. Egoism, by contrast, might seem like virtue.

Altruism might also be divided into two parts: psychological altruism, the theory that people naturally act for the benefit of others, and ethical altruism, the view that they ought to act for the benefit of others. Many theorists have debated whether any of our actions are altruistically motivated, but very few have ever asserted that all of them are. The debate, therefore, typically centers on psychological egoism and the question of whether all our actions are self-interested. Ethical altruism quite naturally runs into questions about the motivation for morality. If we are naturally prone to consider the interests of others and the well-being of society then the egoistic question"Why should I be moral?" loses much of its force. So, too, if reason has its own motivational influence (above and beyond the motivating power of the inclinations, as Kant suggested), then the idea that we always act self-interestedly also loses its initial persuasiveness. It may well be that some of our desires, even our most basic desires, are to be ethical and to help other people when we can. If so, to call the satisfaction of such desires self-interested (much less selfish) is indeed peculiar if not perverse.

The somewhat technical term *egoism* is often confused with the more familiar word *selfishness.* But while egoism entails self-interest, it does not exclude concern for others (just as altruism does not exclude satisfying one's own interests). Selfishness, on the other hand, implies lack of consideration of (or outright interference with) other people and their interests. It is, therefore, not just the pursuit of self-interest but the inconsiderate pursuit of one's own interests.

According to a popular story, President Lincoln was passing a puddle in a carriage when he saw that several piglets were drowning as the mother pig squealed helplessly. He stopped the carriage and saved the piglets. Back on the road, Lincoln's companion asked him whether that act counted as a pure case of altruism. Lincoln replied, "Why, that was the very essence of selfishness. I should have had no peace of mind all day." Lincoln was clearly making a joke, and misusing the word as well.

The word *egoism* may suggest some antagonism between one's own interests and the interests of others. Nevertheless, one can be an egoist and also be charming, morally correct, and even a philanthropist, as a number of very wealthy and ambitious people have demonstrated. The word *selfishness,* however, is another matter. Selfishness implies antagonism between one's own and others' interests, and to say that someone is selfish is to say that the person not only is an egoist but also that he or she subverts the interests of others. *Selfishness* has an undeniable connotation of condemnation and should not be confused with the more neutral term *egoism*. To suggest that everyone's behavior is motivated by self-interest is at least a plausible hypothesis; to suggest that everyone's behavior is selfish is both offensive and implausible. Accordingly, Lincoln's reply to his friend is a bit of nonsense. Satisfying oneself is not the same as being selfish, and even if most human action is (at least in part) self-interested, it is not therefore selfish as well.

Why Be Moral? Self-interest, Motivation, and Justification

Many of the problems that arise in our thinking about morality are the product of an overly sharp dichotomy between the demands of morality and self-interest. Morality is said to be disinterested, while self-interest is obviously interested. Moral rules have some sort of universality and apply to everyone, but self-interest is distinctively particular, concerned with a single person, oneself. We have already noted that the sharp opposition between morality and self-interest leads to a problem of motivation, namely, if it is true that people do only what they want to do and act only according to their own interests, then why could or should people ever act against their interests, as morality may sometimes require? To take our opening example, why should one pay back a debt just because morality demands it? An apostle of self-interest might insist that the reason for repaying the debt was not the sense of obligation (which would be a distinctively moral motive) but, rather, the personal pain of guilt and the annoyance of those nagging thoughts. Or the debt might have been paid with an eye to future possible loans. In other words, despite any noble appearances, the act was self-interested. Indeed, the apostle might say, all actions, no matter how moral or heroic or apparently generous, are motivated by self-interest. We may continue to distinguish, the apostle might allow, between moral appearances and self-interest, but we should understand that all actions are ultimately self-interested.

This sharp opposition between morality and self-interest has danger-ous implications. In a society that preaches the virtues of self-reliance and "looking out for number one," the assumption of self-interest be-comes more than a theory of moral motivation; it becomes a rationale for selfish and immoral behavior as well. In our opening scenario, this view had its explosive but short-lived expression in the table-bashing declaration, "The only person I have to worry about is me!" But in the competitive world of business and professional careers, as well as the "all's fair" worlds of professional sports, love, and war, this rationale can lead to an outright rejection of moral rules, and a world in which human behavior becomes, in the words of the seventeenth-century phi-losopher Thomas Hobbes, "a war of all against all." It is a world in which life becomes "nasty, brutish and short," a "jungle" in which the only rule is survival of the strongest.

It is a mistake, however, to present the opposition between morality and self-interest as an inevitable conflict. Most of the time, because of mutual interests, considerations of reputation, the threat of punishment, and painful pangs of conscience, our interests tend to coincide with our moral obligations. And indeed, if they did not, we could rearrange soci-ety, with systematic rewards and more rigorous, efficient punishment, in such a way that individual interests would almost always coincide with social and moral principles. But this would be an extreme measure and assumes that people are basically self-interested and will cooperate and obey the rules only if they are, essentially, forced to do so. A much more amiable suggestion is that people are naturally social and sociable and are prone to behave in whatever ways are admirable or acceptable in their society. They tend to be selfish and act in their own self-interest (to the obvious detriment of others) only when they are taught or forced to do so by an excessive emphasis on competition to the detriment of cooperation or by conditions of scarcity or adversity that make cooperation impossible. But even in extreme emergency conditions people often act with great courage and generosity; they do not become more antagonistic but more cooperative. The idea that people are naturally self-interested, antagonistic, and accept moral constraints only when forced to do so seems to give us a false picture of human nature, and so too a false picture of morality.

We can imagine a world in which moral action and self-interest would always agree, if society were arranged so that people were rewarded for doing beneficial and socially productive deeds, if they were thoroughly socialized as members of the community and educated in civic participation and, where this failed, if the penalties were such that immoral or antisocial action would always be against one's self-interests. This would still not eliminate the distinction between morality and self-interest, perhaps, and one might insist that the behavior in question, however much in accordance with morality, nonetheless fell short of moral behavior. From a very strict (Kantian) moral point of view, to be moral requires the intention to be moral for its own sake, and this entails at least minimal resistance to one's inclinations. And, of course, it is not moral if one wants only to reap rewards or avoid punishments or censure. To borrow Kant's much-quoted example, a grocer who doesn't cheat his customers just because he is afraid of getting caught cannot be counted as a moral example. He is concerned only with staying in business.

A distinctively moral action seems to require something more than self-interest. Thus Kant tells us that an action has "moral worth" only insofar as it is motivated by duty alone. The motivation of morality thus becomes a key question in ethics, a matter of extreme practical as well as theoretical importance. The question of motivation leads quickly to a the larger question of *justification:* "Why be moral?" If moral actions are not (entirely) self-interested, what reasons and arguments can we give for the moral thesis that people ought sometimes to act against their own self-interest? On the one hand, the question can be construed as "How is it in my interest to be moral?" On the other hand, it can be construed as "How can moral rules be rationally supported, even in the absence of self-interest?" What makes moral action right?

The problem of justification is to show the ultimate correctness of our moral rules. Minimally, the justification of an action is a demonstration that it is (was) the best thing to do in a certain set of circumstances. Ideally, such a demonstration would also show that it was objectively the right thing to do, backed up by the right reasons. One part of the justification of an act might be its contribution to self-interest, and we might also be encouraged to learn that other people did or would have done the same thing, but neither of these is sufficient as justification. Self-interested acts are justified only if they do not violate certain moral constraints, for example, respect for the rights of others; the comment that "everyone is doing it" is a thin justification if the action in question is clearly wrong. But what more do we need to justify an action? The most obvious answer is the existence of some moral rule that permits or commands one kind of action and forbids or prohibits others. To justify an action one might point to a duty or obligation. Or one might state that the action benefits as many people and harms as few as possible. Or one might point out that the course of action (as opposed to any number of others) is fair, or at least, as close to fair as possible. Notice that all of these attempts at justification appeal to some form of objectivity—a moral rule, an obligation, a measurable difference in benefits and harms, some standard of fairness (such as "Each person should get the same" or "Each person should get what he or she deserves"). Some people, however, would argue that moral rules, measurements of help and harm, and standards for fairness are never really objective—even if they are presented as such. Thus we meet the *moral skeptic*, who doubts that any ethical code can be justified. To the skeptic, all morality is ultimately arbitrary, convenient perhaps, and appropriately relative to different societies. But it cannot be justified and cannot be shown to be objectively correct or defensible by dispassionate reason. The great eighteenth-century moral skeptic David Hume argues that morality is just a matter of "sentiments," some of which are universal and natural but which are not rational and not rationally justifiable. But Hume, we should note, was a perfect gentleman of his times, and the fact that he thought morality to be unjustifiable did not seem to affect his behavior at all. The moral skeptic doubts or denies the possibility of justification, but accepts morality nonetheless. A more dangerous character is the *amoralist,* a person who acts without regard for generally accepted moral principles, and worse yet is the *immoralist,* who recognizes those principles but conscientiously disobeys them. Both the amoralist and the immoralist are sometimes called *nihilists,* who not only deny the justifiability of morality but refuse to accept its dictates as well. Happily, however, very few people are either amoralists or immoralists, but their very possibility has provoked philosophers to pursue their quest for an adequate justification of morality. Whether or not philosophers can convince the nihilists to change their ways, at least they can prove that the nihilists are wrong about the status of morality.

Acting for Reasons: Two Kinds of Theories

The key to morality and its justification is that we do not just act; we act for reasons. Indeed, it is the very nature of human action that it is *intentional,* which means that it is done (1) with a purpose and (2) for reasons. Whether or not we have an intention in mind before acting (an articulate thought concerning what we are going to do), our actions are nevertheless intentional. To say that our actions are rational is, minimally, to say that they have an intelligible purpose, and this purpose can (usually) be stated more or less clearly and without hesitation as a reason for action. Only in the exceptional case do we have to ponder the difficult question, "Why did I do that?" (Under the prodding of a psychoanalyst or philosopher, of course, one might well become confused about his or her motivation for even the most ordinary actions. But usually our reasons for acting are transparent even if they remain unstated.)

Dogs may act with a purpose, of course. Fido scratches at the screen door in order to attract attention and be let out. But dogs do not act for reasons in the sense that is relevant to ethics, and, accordingly, even the best-behaved dog does not deserve to be called moral. It is not just that reasons in ethics should be articulate, thus requiring language. Rather, reasons require Reason, which is to say, a complex of reasons beyond the immediate notion of "do this to get that." Reasoning requires abstraction, reflection, and the need to justify one's course of action. A college woman with the ambition to be a federal judge someday has to think ahead years or decades, not just about wanting to get into law school. She has to think in terms of her education, her credentials, her reputation, her choice of friends, the way she will spend her summers. And of course she must have a concept of the law and the legal system.

There is nothing in this complex of reasons that need be particularly moral, of course. Indeed, the young woman's ambition may have wholly to do with her own vision of herself. But such an ambition is a clear example of how conceptually rich it is to act intentionally. To act for reasons means that the question of justification is relevant and important. It is not just an annoying addendum that philosophers have added to human action; it is part and parcel of human action as such. We would be shocked, to say the least, if the question, "Why do you want to go to law school?" were answered simply by "Oh, I have no idea whatever" or "It just sounds like fun." Actions have reasons, and these reasons in turn have reasons. One applies to law school to get into law school, which one does in order to become a lawyer, which one does in order, perhaps, to enter politics, make money, join one's mother's law firm, and so on. Ethics, then, can be considered the study of our reasons.

Reasoning and justification must have an end, however. There must be a final purpose, or what the ancient Greeks (notably Aristotle) called a *telos*. A chain of reasons needs to be anchored; the network of reasons has to be hung somewhere. One might say, for example that the ultimate reason for going to law school, or for doing anything, for that matter, is to be happy. Or to get more pleasure out of life. Or to become as powerful or as popular as possible. If the skeptic returns with another unreasonable question, such as "Why do you want to be happy?" we seem stuck for an answer. Perhaps we can mumble something like "It's just human nature to want to be happy" or "Well, everyone wants to be happy." But, again, we have the feeling that the question is unreasonable. One does not, after all, question ultimate ends, and certainly not happiness.

The above candidates for the position of ultimate end of action and anchor for our reasons are, whatever their differences, all of a kind. They are all ultimate purposes, desirable ends in themselves toward which all our other actions and reasons are aimed. But there is another kind of reason, and another kind of end point to our reasoning. "It's the right thing to do." "It's my duty to do so." "God wills it." How are these reasons different from those mentioned previously? For one thing, ethicists would point out, they are not personal reasons in the way that happiness, pleasure, popularity, and power are; they specify considerations that are independent of people's wants or desires. They are moral reasons, that is, they presuppose an understanding of moral concepts such as *right* and *wrong, good* and *evil, moral* and *immoral, ought,* and *obligation.* Such reasons are involved in many of our actions, whether or not we are called upon to justify ourselves. That fact is not challenged even by the moral skeptic, who would agree that we (and people in most cultures) employ such reasons and act according to them. The skeptical challenge, rather, is aimed at the ultimate justification of such reasons, that is, the idea that the chain of moral reasons can be anchored in some objective truth or principle.

Most of us, however, including the moral skeptic, would be quite willing to continue in our quest for happiness, or perhaps even pleasure, or popularity, or power, even if we were not convinced that there was any ultimate purpose in doing so. But this willingness is not so clear in cases where morality itself is the end. We are moral, presumably, because we assume that there is some higher reason for being so than our own personal well-being. If morality does not lead to personal well-being and if those higher reasons are indeed unjustifiable, there may be no answer to the question, ''Why be moral?''

The quest for justification is answered by theories of morality. A moral theory is not just an attempt to describe or explain the phenomenon of morality (as a theory in the natural or social sciences would). It is an attempt to justify morality, to provide the anchor for moral reasons. Using a different metaphor, many philosophers, especially Kant, have spoken of ''grounding'' morality, that is, building a rational foundation upon which all our reasons can then be combined in a single coherent structure. But, as we have noted two different kinds of reasons for actions and two different kinds of anchors or groundings, so too we have two different kinds of theories of morality, corresponding to the two senses of justification. Morality may be justified by showing that it has its own moral end point; this ultimate reason is more fundamental than any personal or collective goals we might have, including happiness. Or, morality may be justified by showing that it leads, ultimately, to the attainment of personal and collective goals, such as happiness. But in this latter case moral reasons are not themselves the ultimate reasons. Morality is a means to something else, such as happiness or social well-being.

Moral philosophers have traditionally given two rather formidable names to these two kinds of theories. Theories of morality that claim that morality provides its own ultimate anchor or grounding are called *deontological* (from the Greek word *deon,* for "duty"). Theories of morality that place some nonmoral purpose at the end of moral reasoning are called *teleological* (from the Greek word *telos,* meaning "purpose"). We will examine several varieties of these theories in the following chapter.

Rules and Virtues

In our introduction to ethics, we have so far followed an established Kantian tradition by placing a special emphasis on morality and moral *principles.* Indeed, our ethical tradition is built around the importance of formally stated rules, from the Ten Commandments in the Old Testament to the policy of "government of laws, not men" put into practice by the framers of the United States Constitution. But this emphasis on principles is not the whole of ethics, and there are many systems of ethics which do not stress principles at all. For example, in some societies the central concern of ethics is obedience, to a ruler or a religious leader, for example, and general principles of the sort we have been discussing may not enter into their system of ethics. One could always formulate the principle, "Do whatever he or she says!" but this is a dubious example of a moral principle. The nature of ethics as well as its specific content is also a matter of ethos, and not all ethé are so bound up with what we call morality.

What is essential to ethics might not be universal rules and objective rational principles but rather an established way of doing things, a shared sense of value and significance. Consider a group of children at play, throwing a ball or chasing each other through the woods. Their game does not necessarily need rules. In fact, one might suggest, children tend to formulate rules for activities only when things start to get out of hand. For example, one of the children may decide to sit on the ball and not let the others have it. Consequently the others formulate a "no sitting on the ball" rule. What is essential for understanding almost all human activities is not so much the notion of a rule as such but the idea of a *practice,* a shared cooperative activity with mutually understood goals, whether competitive, cooperative, or individual. Most practices have rules, but rules are not what define the practice. Consider, for example, almost any game. The object of a game may be as simple as keeping a ball in motion or as complicated as the trading games that are daily played on Wall Street. A game has its champions, whom both players and spectators admire, and modes of behavior that are unacceptable and punishable, even if no one has ever bothered to prohibit them in a rule. So, too, a society has goals, perhaps the happiness and prosperity of all of its citizens, but military might, prestige, or religious orthodoxy may also be goals, whether they are conducive to happiness and prosperity or not. A society has heroes and idols whom the citizens seek to emulate—the self-made millionaire in a primarily business society, the warrior-chieftain in a primarily military society, the spiritual leader in a primarily religious society. And a society may or may not have formal rules. It is sometimes suggested that certain social activities work best without formal rules or laws. For example, business people decry government regulation and insist that the business world works best when left to its own nonmoral governance by supply and demand. And artists often defy social convention and rules.

In our preliminary characterization of morality, we said that many theorists insist that morality consists of rules, principles, and laws; it is not merely right action but right action on principle. If we accept this characterization of ethics, we might have to conclude that examples of games, societies, and activities without rules are devoid of ethical concern, even though they clearly have standards of behavior and ideals. In business, for example, participants share understandings about what is fair and what is not, and a great deal of business is conducted based on verbal agreements, mutual trust, and cooperation. So too are most of our relationships and dealings with other people. There is much to ethics that is not necessarily a matter of principle.

Activities that are not based on explicit rules or principles are not amoral. The ancient Greeks, for instance, would not have understood our emphasis on rules and principles. They were far more concerned with the *virtues* and the *character* of individuals. Obeying the laws of society was more or less taken for granted, but a good person was not just someone who obeyed the rules. Such people also displayed personal traits and exceptional abilities, characteristics which involved much more than simply abstaining from evil. Indeed, a Homeric Greek with many warrior virtues might indulge in a great many dubious deeds and nevertheless remain an ethical hero. Greek ethics turned on individual virtue and heroism more than on obedience and principled behavior.

Largely because of the influence of the great German philosopher Immanuel Kant, however, the emphasis in ethics in the past two hundred years has shifted to the specific nature of morality as a set of universal principles. But, although we might expect to find rules of some kind in any articulate civilization, it would be a mistake to think of rules alone as the key to ethics. Character and the characteristics of particular individuals are as important as obedience to rules. For example, the virtues of compassion, generosity, courage, and so on are an important part of morals, but they do not consist of following rules. Moral behavior in this sense is often spontaneous, habitual, and unthinking, while morality in the Kantian sense places a premium on being deliberative, thoughtful, and reflective. This emphasis on character also allows us to focus on what is special about a person. There is no reason to expect that all admirable people will be the same.

This shift from morality as obedience and rules to character has its problematic aspects. One of the more intriguing complications of the introduction of the virtues into ethics is the complicated moral status of people who don't obey the rules but nevertheless emerge as heroes of a sort. One notable example is the *rogue*. Some rogues, such as Robin

Hood might be morally defended as appealing to a higher morality than the laws of the land. But many of the heroes in American movies, for example, have no such thought in mind. They may simply be asserting their own freedom or having a good time. They are chased by the police, and they do such things as wreck cars and rob banks. They even betray their friends, yet they retain our admiration because of the characters they are. On the more respectable side of the law, too, we find general admiration for the rogue. For example, one type of social hero today is the *entrepreneur,* the maverick businessperson who takes high risks in order to get a new idea or product on the market. One professor at the Harvard Business School recently wrote that to understand the entrepreneur you have to understand the mind of a juvenile delinquent. Many of our most popular artists and musicians are admired despite what would seem to be their dubious morals. So the question, "What virtues are to count?" becomes central to the issue of virtue ethics. Are there specifically moral virtues, and if so, could it be that virtue ethics is nothing but morality-in-action, moral rules internalized and cultivated as habit? Then the distinction between two kinds of ethics collapses and morality retains its central place. Or is it the case that the virtues cannot be reduced to morality-in-action? In part 3 of this book, we will see some reasons for thinking that virtue complements traditional notions about morality.

The History of Ethics: Ten Great Moral Philosophers

Our ethics as well as our ethos is derived from a long tradition, stretching back in history to ancient times. Foremost among the books and authors that have influenced us, of course, is the Bible and its many scribes and speakers. But of nearly equal importance are the mores and opinions of the ancient peoples of Greece and Rome as well as dozens of other ethnic groups whose views on life have slowly evolved into our own.

In philosophy, however, the history of ethics is punctuated, if not actually defined by a number of truly great moral philosophers who wrote about the mores and morals of their own societies and, at the same time, tried to say something universal about morality and living the good life. Even a survey of the history of ethics would include several dozen such authors, and a detailed study would take many years and include possibly hundreds or thousands of minor moralists, essayists, theologians, social reformers, political theorists, and newspaper editors. Here we have included several names that have repeatedly appeared in our discussion and will continue to do so for the remainder of the book. What follows is a brief introduction to ten of the most influential moral philosophers in Western history:

Socrates and Plato
Aristotle
Saint Augustine
Thomas Hobbes
David Hume
Immanuel Kant
John Stuart Mill
Friedrich Nietzsche
Jean-Paul Sartre

Socrates and Plato

Socrates lived from 470 until 399 B.C. His student Plato lived from 427 to 347 B.C. Most of what we know of Socrates's ethical teachings comes to us through Plato's writings, in which Socrates's conversations or "dialogues" with other Greek philosophers are preserved in vivid, dramatic form. In Plato's earliest dialogues, Socrates's story and his teachings are carefully preserved for us. Against the Sophists who taught such pessimistic theses as "All men are selfish" and "There is no such thing as justice," Socrates took a positive and optimistic view, exemplifying his own integrity and arguing against injustice. Of particular importance is Socrates's insistence on dialogue and debate, "the examined life," as he called it. Socrates spent his life arguing the importance of living virtuously. In his early seventies, he was accused of corrupting the youth with his teaching. He was tried and executed. After his death, Plato established the Academy in Athens for the purpose of continuing Socrates's work. In Plato's later dialogues, he clearly embellished Socrates's views and insisted that, over and above the changing things of this world, there was a pure world of "Forms," including the pure Forms of Justice and the Good.

Aristotle

Aristotle was born in 384 B.C. in northern Greece. His father was the physician of King Philip of Macedonia, and Aristotle later became tutor to the king's son, Alexander (soon to become "the Great"). Aristotle studied with Plato for eighteen years, but he also became the world's most accomplished scientist. His theories of biology and physics influenced Western science for almost two thousand years. In ethics, he developed a theory that was very much in the spirit of biology. Everything, including all human activity, he argued, has a purpose or function, a *telos.* The ultimate human purpose is happiness, but happiness is not just a life filled with pleasures and satisfactions. It must also be a rational life, a life in accordance with reason. And it must be an active and a virtuous life, "a life of rational activity in accordance with virtue."

Saint Augustine

Augustine was born in Africa in A.D. 354. He was not religious as a young man but in his thirties, while in Rome, he embraced Christianity and became one of the most influential voices in the development of Christian ethics and theology. Following Plato's and Socrates's vision of the "pure Form of the Good," which he interpreted as God, Augustine argued that Christian ethics requires the separation of the secular and the divine. In opposition to Aristotle, Augustine insisted that the purpose of life is religious faith and salvation.

Thomas Hobbes

Hobbes was born in England in 1588. He graduated from Oxford University and entered into a lifetime of study in mathematics, philosophy, and science. (One of his friends was Galileo.) His philosophical writings were politically controversial and got him into trouble. He escaped to France, but his irreligious writings got him in even more trouble there, and he fled back to England, where he wrote his greatest book, *The Leviathan*. The book is a masterful political treatise in which Hobbes attacks the ancient idea of "the divine right of kings" and replaces it with the radical view that societies are based on a "social contract" between everyone in the society. As the basis of this theory, however, Hobbes also argues his famous thesis that all men are naturally selfish and that, in the "state of nature," before men enter into the social contract, human life is "nasty, brutish and short," "a war of all against all."

David Hume

Hume was born in Scotland in 1711. He was an atheist and a self-proclaimed "pagan" whose theory of human nature was an attempt to return to the ethics of the Greeks, Aristotle in particular, in which happiness and social utility were of the greatest importance. Accordingly, he attacked Christian virtues, such as humility, which he thought to be degrading. He emphasized the importance of having a virtuous character, which includes the natural feeling or sentiment of sympathy and forms the basis of all ethics. He was skeptical about the traditional emphasis on reason in ethics, suggesting that "reason is and ought to be the slave of the passions." Because of his atheism and skepticism, Hume was never able to teach philosophy in the universities, and some of his books were condemned.

Immanuel Kant

Kant was born in eastern Prussia in 1724. He was a pious Lutheran, and his ethical philosophy reflects his Christian sense of morality. The key to his thinking about ethics is that morality is essentially a matter of "practical reason," and "universal law," or what he calls the "categorical imperative." Kant rejected both the idea that moral principles can be securely based on human feelings, or sentiments, and the idea that morals may differ from one society or one time to another. Despite his moral conservatism, however, he remained an ardent enthusiast of the French Revolution of 1789, even through its worst years. And in his great philosophical works, especially three monumental books called *Critiques (The Critique of Pure Reason, The Critique of Practical Reason,* and *The Critique of Judgment),* he set in motion his own powerful revolution in philosophy.

John Stuart Mill

John Stuart Mill was born in 1806 in England. His father, James, was already a famous philosopher who, with Jeremy Bentham, founded the ethical movement known as *utilitarianism.* John Stuart Mill became the movement's most articulate and best-known defender. Utilitarianism is essentially the thesis that a good act is that which results in "the greatest good for the greatest number" of people. It is an ethics that, as the name implies, puts its emphasis on the usefulness, or utility, of actions in making people happy, or at least in not making them more miserable. It is an ethics that places far more emphasis on the good or bad consequences of an action than it does on the intentions according to which the action is carried out. Thus, Mill and Kant are often cast as the central opponents in many contemporary arguments in ethics.

Friedrich Nietzsche

Nietzsche was born in 1844 in a small town in Germany. He spent most of his life, however, in Italy and Switzerland, and he liked to call himself a "good European." He was trained in the classics and loved the life of the ancient Greeks, which he compared unflatteringly with nineteenth-century life. Accordingly, his ethical philosophy consists mainly of a virulent attack on Judeo-Christian morality and its religious supports. He proclaimed that "God is dead" (that is, people no longer believed in him) and, given that ominous fact, the morals of our society would soon collapse as well. What we call morality, Nietzsche argued, is in fact just a weapon of the weak that is used to bring everyone to the same level. Unlike most modern moralists, Nietzsche was an unabashed *elitist,* insisting that all people are not equal. Some people are superior, he maintained, and rather than follow the rules of the herd they should follow their virtues. His ethics, according to his imaginary spokesman Zarathustra, is for a few, for those who find themselves unhealthily inhibited by the strictures of morality and who have much more to offer the world than mere good citizenship.

Jean-Paul Sartre

Sartre was born in Paris in 1905. He is generally recognized as the definitive spokesperson for the philosophy known as *existentialism,* which he expounded in his mammoth wartime work *Being and Nothingness,* begun while he was in a German prison camp. The central theme of his ethics is the concept of freedom. "We are condemned to be free," he writes in his usual dramatic manner. He rejects such ideas as our natural purpose is happiness or that we are naturally selfish. There is no human nature, he says, except for the fact of our freedom. We are what we make of ourselves, Sartre argues, and by the same reasoning, there are no moral laws or principles of reason which bind us all. Our morals are what we decide to do, and our principles are those which we choose to act upon. In accordance with this philosophy, Sartre was an ardent political reformer, committed to many causes. He was offered but refused the Nobel Prize. He died in 1980 at the age of 75.

TWO

Doing the Right Thing: The Nature of Morality

From a practical point of view, ethics might simply be summarized as doing the right thing. Even before we begin to think about theories or the enormous variety of examples and cases that are suggested by doing the right thing, most people feel quite comfortable with this basic idea. If you make a promise, you ought to keep it. If you borrow money, you ought to return it. If you are reporting on a situation, you ought to tell the truth. If you are taking a test, you ought not to cheat. And so on. Ethics begins, as Aristotle told us, with a good up-bringing, and much of this upbringing consists of being taught, in hundreds if not thousands of particular cases, what is the right thing (and what is the wrong thing) to do. But these lessons are not all of equal importance or of the same kind. There is a difference between being taught a nuance of courtesy and being told not to hurt other people. There is a difference between being taught something for your own good and being told to do something because it is your duty or an obligation. And it is in the attempt to understand these differences that ethics and education in ethics moves from a collection of cultivated behavioral responses to an understanding of the underlying principles and practices of morality.

What makes such understanding necessary, in part, is the fact that we often find ourselves in situations in which what we have been taught is not sufficient, either because the situation is new to us, because we do not know how to predict the consequences, because it lies in a gray area in which it is not evident which of several responses is appropriate, or because it involves an actual conflict between two (or more) very different responses. For example, we are told to tell the truth in response to a question, and we are taught not to hurt people if it can be avoided. But the conjunction of these two sometimes leads to a contradiction, when, for example, answering a question truthfully will result in harm that might otherwise be avoided. To take a simple case, a friend who has just gotten a ghastly haircut asks you, "How do I look?" Or, much more serious, the leader of a lynch mob asks you if you know where your (falsely accused) friend is hiding. The possibility of novel situations requires some general guidelines which go beyond the limited number of contexts in which one has been ethically educated, and the frequency of gray areas requires the ability to reason about what one has learned in order to capture the spirit of the ethical prescriptions rather than unthinkingly following instructions. The inevitability of conflicts and uncertainties in ethics means that one must learn not just what to do in this or that particular case and not just some guidelines or principles, but one needs a set of priorities and a way of thinking about them.

The most common conflicts are those between one's own self-interest and the dictates of morality. On the one hand, you may really want to do something; on the other hand, it is immoral. Or, on the one side, you see a clear path to fulfilling a lifelong ambition; on the other, you would have to lie, cheat, steal, or betray a friend in order to take that path. Doing the right thing does not always or even usually involve acting against your own best interests, but it sometimes does, such as when you find that keeping a promise you made some time ago has become extremely inconvenient or expensive. Indeed, even when one's self-interest clearly coincides with what one ought to do, we often make a distinction between doing what one ought to do because it is the right thing to do and doing it just because what is right happens to be in one's self-interest. Thus it is important to distinguish the morally right thing to do from what is simply prudent. But then again, the moral skeptic might well ask why one should ever act contrary to his or her own self-interests—unless, of course, doing so (in the short run) will serve one's longer-term interests. If the aim and justification of morality were just to serve our ultimate self-interest, then such cases as the above would suggest—what is intolerable—that it is alright to be immoral if it is in one's better interests.

The question, What is morality and how is it justified? has become one of the leading questions of ethics. In the introduction, we pointed out that morality and moral rules were distinguished by their importance and priority, by their universality, rationality, and objectivity, and by their unselfish concern for others. But even within these guidelines (which are themselves often a matter of some dispute, as we shall see) there is ample room for alternative interpretations and justifications. In this chapter, we shall see that there are quite a few distinctive theories of morality, all of them in at least partial conflict with each other and none of them entirely adequate by itself. Some are concerned primarily with explaining the *authority* of morality, that is, the power or right of morality to command our obedience, even when its dictates are contrary to our interests. Others are concerned primarily with making the connection between self-interest, personal happiness, and the public good. Some are concerned primarily with emphasizing the special rational and objective status of morality, while others are out to reduce morality to less honorable motives and undermine its special importance. Indeed, whether all of these theories deserve to be called theories of morality is itself an essential part of the debate, for the reasons we discussed in part 1. Does morality require obedience, and if so, to what or to whom? Is morality compatible with self-interest and conducive to the public good? Under what conditions and in what circumstances? What does it mean to say that morality or moral rules are objective? And is there any special domain of human behavior and concern that deserves to be called moral? These are some of the questions we will examine in part 2.

Doing the Right Thing: The Example of Socrates

If you were to face an ultimate conflict between obedience to morality and your own happiness, which would you choose? Suppose you knew that doing the right thing could cost you your life. No situation provides a more indisputable test of one's ultimate values than a life-or-death decision.

In the history of philosophy, the most dramatic example of this ultimate moral test is the case of Socrates, the great Greek philosopher and teacher who was condemned to death in ancient Athens. In 399 B.C. Socrates was already an old man over 70, but he had made a considerable reputation (and a nuisance of himself) by challenging the favorite assumptions of the leading politicians of the city. He had also made many enemies and, finally, was accused of corrupting the minds of the young students who flocked around him. After a lengthy and famous trial, he was sentenced to die by drinking hemlock, a deadly poison that causes great pain and violent convulsions before taking its final effect. In his trial (reported to us in Plato's dialogue *Apology*) Socrates defends philosophy and attacks the unsound opinions of the *hoi polloi,* the mass of ordinary citizens. He maintains his innocence and argues that the charge is unjust. He even suggests to the jury that he should receive a pension instead of punishment. But despite his eloquence, the jury decided against him, and Socrates was sent off to prison to await his execution.

In prison, however, Socrates had the opportunity to escape. His friend Crito came to him and reported that Socrates's many friends and admirers had already lined up a number of crucial bribes and escape routes as well as a safe haven for Socrates in exile. His family and friends would be with him and, still in exceptional health, he would be able to look forward to at least several more years of happiness. But Socrates, in Plato's dialogue *Crito,* produces an argument that has been immensely unsettling to philosophers and philosophy students ever since. The pursuit of happiness and the injustice of the sentence are not enough to justify his escaping, he argues with Crito, who becomes increasingly upset with his seemingly stubborn teacher. Reason tells him that what he ought to do is to stay and be executed; his personal pleasures are not ultimately important, he insists. The injustice of the sentence and the abuse of the law are not grounds for disobeying and rejecting the law itself. One can defy authorities, as Socrates often did, but one is still bound by reason and law.

Socrates's argument begins by insisting that personal considerations—one's emotions and desires—must not determine one's course of action. Reason must do that. Furthermore, Socrates several times rejects Crito's argument that virtually everyone thinks that Socrates would be right to escape. "We should not care what people in general think," he insists. The only consideration is what is right, and reason alone will tell us this. And what is right, Socrates goes on to argue, is to act for the good of one's "soul." This means, he argues, to obey the laws of the state even when they are unjust. Not to do so would be to betray oneself, as well as to weaken the power of the laws by making oneself an exception (and thereby encouraging others to do so too). By remaining in Athens, Socrates continues, he has agreed, in effect, to obey its laws, and now he has an obligation to continue to do so, even when those laws turn against him. It is doing good itself that is his ultimate concern. Nevertheless, Socrates concludes, in respecting the law he is also doing what is best for himself and everyone else. The best way to live is to always do the right thing, even if doing the right thing undermines the pleasures of life, or life itself.

Socrates knew that he had done right and had been treated unfairly by the court. He then faced an unenviable choice: to turn down the offer to escape and face death or to leave Athens for sanctuary elsewhere and live the rest of his life with the knowledge that he had violated his trust and done wrong. He chose to stay and be executed on the ground that there are matters more important than even life itself. That which is most worth living for may also be worth dying for.

If you had been in Socrates's position, what would you have done? If you had decided to escape, how would you defend your decision against someone who accused you of violating your own moral principles by flouting the law? What are the implications of your answer?

Morality and the Law: The Problem of Authority

Socrates's decision to face execution rather than to escape and continue his happy life made him the most celebrated philosophical hero of all times and a champion of the moral life. But the motivation behind Socrates's decision was by no means obvious, nor indeed was the nature of the decision itself. On the one hand, he clearly argues that one has an obligation to obey the law of the land and accept the authority of the state, even where the result is injustice. On the other hand, obeying the law of the land as such was not Socrates's highest priority, and it was not for the sake of the laws of Athens that he died. In *Apology,* he argues quite emphatically (as Jesus and his followers would argue several centuries later) that the Good is above the law and that there are circumstances in which one should conscientiously break the law, as Socrates did when he insisted on continuing to teach philosophy despite the official warnings against his doing so. And even in *Crito,* he quite explicitly argues that it is for his own sake, for the sake of his soul, that he is sacrificing his life, not just for the sake of the laws of Athens, with which he often disagreed. But then, what is the relationship between the laws of particular societies and morality? Should we obey the laws only when we find reason to do so but break laws when we disagree with them? Where does our obligation to obey the law come from? Obeying the law in general, would seem to be a moral obligation if anything is. But what gives the laws their authority, and what gives morality its ultimate authority?

If morality is to be something more than mere prudence or the projection of our own personal prejudices onto others, it must have authority. Authority is, first of all, a kind of power, legitimate power, which overrides personal interests and preferences and provides a source of appeal for disputes and disagreements. Socrates, by virtue of his wisdom and (in retrospect) his heroic status had enormous moral authority. But Socrates continually complained about his personal ignorance and always appealed to higher laws, ultimately to the Good itself, to justify his actions and opinions. Indeed, his appeal to the law in *Crito* is just one of many such appeals to higher authority, and his decision to obey the law, even where the law was wrong, was just one more way of emphasizing the relative unimportance of one person's life compared to the Good as such. It is the Good itself, the ultimate ideal that informs everything that we do, that gives authority to all particular acts and decisions as well as to the particular laws of a particular state or society. Good laws are such only insofar as they conform to this ultimate authority.

But what is this ultimate authority, and how does one recognize it? Is there an ultimate ideal that informs everything and everyone everywhere? Many philosophers and a great many jurists and lawyers have backed away from this difficult philosophical question and have attempted instead to rest the case for morality on the local laws of the land. There, at least, we have something explicit, written in black and white, and while we might debate at length about the correct interpretation of a law or whether a law ought to be repealed, at least we know that it is the law and where its authority lies. Its authority lies in the state and in the society as a whole. But is this enough? Some philosophers would argue that what is right is defined and determined by the law, and whatever the law says is obligatory, whether or not there are good reasons for changing the law. But where would these reasons come from, and aren't there considerations outside of the law that weigh on our sense of obligation as heavily as the authority of the law?

The thesis that what is right is defined and determined by the law would seem to follow from the importance of ethos in ethics, for it is the culture as a whole that determines both its own morals and its legal system. Using this fact, many relativists insist that there is no higher ideal or law outside of a culture to which its morals can be appealed. But this is a troubling conclusion. What happens, for example, when a society commits foul crimes against its own citizens? Or when a society has a corrupt, unjust legal system? The world provides examples of bad and even evil societies. Nazi Germany and apartheid South Africa are two frequently cited examples. Furthermore, it is clear that not all citizens of a country agree on many moral matters, even when they agree about the laws which give the society its guidelines. One of the enduring disputes in the philosophy of law is precisely the question of whether one can or should legislate morals, and the very question makes it evident that the power and sanctions of the law of the land are one thing and morals another. Moreover, when one considers the origins of laws—whether in the pronouncements of a dictator, as legislation, or passed by a democratic majority, or as handed down through the ages as tradition—it is clear that there are no guarantees that laws will always be good and several reasons to suppose that, at least sometimes, they might not be. As society changes, laws become out of date. The politics of the moment sometimes overwhelms good moral sense and the law becomes a tangle of impossible demands. A society's legal system and its rules of ethics, including its moral rules, are not the same.

Part of what makes Socrates's arguments and decision so difficult is that in his case the judgment of law is so clearly unfair, even, we might say, immoral. It seems reasonable to argue that it is in general morally right to obey the law, or that one always has an obligation to obey the law except when there is an overwhelming reason not to. But this qualification, even if it applies only rarely, is extremely important. What would not count as an overwhelming reason, of course, is strong personal interest; one is not justified in cheating on one's federal income tax (which would be breaking the law) merely on the grounds that one really needs the money to buy a new sailboat. But one might well have an overwhelming reason to break a particular law if that law seems to contradict some higher principle of morality. Thus, pacifists have refused to pay their taxes on the grounds that taxes are used to fight wars, an activity they consider immoral, and some have even gone to prison rather than fight in a war.

The *Crito* does not give us a clear way of understanding conflicts between morality and the law, but Plato's view of the Good does provide us with an excellent if obscure way of understanding this conflict. The Good, like God, stands above all laws and customs; it therefore provides an absolute standard by which all local laws can be evaluated. For example, many states once had laws allowing slavery and denying even the most basic economic rights to women and children. But the Good, one might argue, includes the demand that all people have rights, including the right to certain minimal freedoms which slavery denies. (It is worth noting, however, that Plato lived in a society that accepted slavery as natural.) Where the law violates our conception of the Good, many good citizens are willing to argue that the moral thing to do is to break the law, while also trying to change them. There are moral ideals and authority above the law of the land, and invoking the Good is convenient for making this point. But what, then, is the Good?

The Good and God's Will

The one fact that almost everyone agrees would have profound authority in moral matters and would justify morality beyond question is the existence of an all-knowing, all-powerful, just, and beneficent God. One need not say that the words *good* and *ought* mean "commanded by God," but it is clear that the notion of the Good would be clarified and the quest for justification would be solved if we could know that certain things are good and right because God commands them.

One problem is that we don't seem to know with any certainty exactly what it is that God commands. The Bible is not a document written in a single voice. The Old and New Testaments depict God and his behavior quite differently and, consequently, they offer us different conceptions of morality. Even within each testament there are a number of different views of morality. At the risk of gross oversimplification, we might mention, for example, that the God of the Old Testament is sometimes introduced as a jealous and at times a wrathful God who nevertheless watches over his chosen people and assures them victory in battle. Elsewhere in the Old Testament, God tests his people, allows their temples and their homeland to be destroyed, and sometimes (as in the story of Job) subjects his people to excruciating torments. The God of the New Testament is celebrated rather as a loving God who is not so concerned with punishing his people as with saving them through his own sacrifice. Even the Gospels give us significantly different portraits of Christ, which have given rise to very different interpretations of the meaning of God and Christianity as a whole. The ethical visions that emerge from these two basic conceptions of God differ accordingly. The Old Testament emphasizes obedience to God's law. The New Testament takes as its highest commandment that we should love one another. (While these ethical views are not incompatible (one can be loving and obedient at the same time), they are signigicantly different.)

While it may be difficult to use the Bible to answer day-to-day questions about behavior, there is no question that the Bible provides us with a general conception and justification of morality. We may disagree on what the Bible says about opening shops on the Sabbath or working mothers, but there is no disagreement about its prohibitions of murder, stealing, and adultery.

Many people attempt to bypass problems of Biblical interpretation by appealing directly to personal faith and individual conscience—to the presence of God within or a feeling of God in one's heart. One need not doubt or belittle the importance of such religious feelings and promptings in order to question their dependability as a source of moral directives and justification. How does one know that the promptings of one's heart or conscience are indeed the will of God? History is full of insane people who have felt such promptings acutely and had no doubts about their divine origin. Most likely, we know that the promptings of our conscience are good because they conform to the morality taught in the Bible. Thus we do not interpret the occasional urge to kill as a divine message, as we do the quiet urge to forgive someone.

Even if one ignores questions of interpretation and accepts without question the idea that the Bible is the literal, revealed word of God, difficult questions confront the most faithful believer. There are certain commandments and descriptions of the acts of God in the Bible—for example, God's order to Abraham to kill his son and God's treatment of Job—that demand a justification. Family murder and wanton cruelty to the innocent are actions which we find morally intolerable. God on occasion wipes out entire populations by fire or flood, presumably including a number of innocent children. And even apart from these acts of Biblical vengeance, we can think of hundreds of natural disasters, or "acts of God"—hurricanes, floods, and earthquakes—in which the innocent have perished. What are we to make of such horrible events? Are God's actions and commands always moral?

In the long history of discussion of this question, three primary answers have been embraced. The first answer is that if God did or commanded these things, they are good without any qualification. The second answer is that these acts, which seem to us to be very evil, are in fact good. They are an example of "God's mysterious ways." The third response is that these acts are immoral and that not everything that God does or commands is good. (There is a fourth answer, of course, which eliminates the question, which is to insist that there is no God or, that even if there were a God he would make no difference to morality.)

The first answer reflects a straightforward acceptance of the thesis that God's will defines the Good. If God does something out of line with what we call morality, what he does is nevertheless good. This view raises a problem, however, for if one accepts these biblical accounts, one will conclude that God does not always insist on what we call morality. Of course, we can and do revise our sense of morality to fit with our interpretation of the Bible and our experience, so this should be seen as a dynamic interpretive process, not just a matter of simple agreement or disagreement. Nevertheless, we may be uncomfortable with the idea that whatever God does or directs is therefore good, for this makes it impossible to even raise the question whether God would or could do wrong.

The second answer allows one to keep both the view that what God wills is good and the thesis that God justifies morality. That is its perennial appeal. The problem raised by the second answer is how God's sometimes brutal biblical behavior can be understood as moral. By appealing to "mysterious ways" one might save faith but would lose the direct and obvious connection between God and morality. To say that something is a mystery is not to explain or understand it, but rather to insist that one cannot explain or understand it. This view seems to require some independent conception of morality that we can use to show that God's will is in accordance with it.

The third and last answer accepts the conclusion that there is a difference between God, God's will, and morality, but this interpretation means that we give up the idea that God alone can justify morality. We must have some independent conception and justification of morality, which may or may not apply to God as well. The third answer openly embraces this view, where the second seems to be forced into it. Of course, almost anyone who believes in the traditional Judeo-Christian God will also believe that God does in fact only good. But to believe that he does so in fact and not by definition is an important difference. While one wants to believe that God is good, it hardly serves as a proof to simply define whatever God does as good.

The conclusion that we have to know what is good apart from our belief in God goes back as far as Plato. In a dialogue called *Euthyphro,* he considers the question of whether something is good or right because the gods command it, or whether the gods command it because it is good or right. Socrates quickly convinces Euthyphro of the latter position, which means that what is good is good apart from the fact that the gods will it. Even if one is not troubled by the examples in the Bible, one can consider the following hypothetical situation. Suppose someone were to uncover what seemed to be an authentic original manuscript from the Bible that gave us a perverse set of commandments, such as "Thou shalt kill," "Thou shalt steal," and "Thou shalt commit adultery as much as thou wouldst." Would we not reject the manuscript, its apparent authenticity aside, just because of our conviction that God would not command such immorality? But that means that we have a conception of morality that does not depend wholly on God's will; to the contrary, we are confident that God wills us to be moral because we believe that God himself is a moral being.

The idea that God is the authority upon which morality is based need not mean that morality is justified because God wills it. It has often been suggested that God justifies morality because he sanctions it, that is, he sees to it that those who are moral are (eventually) rewarded and that those who are evil are (eventually) punished. This assurance is perfectly compatible with the idea that morality is quite independent of God's will. This view of God as a sanctioning agent provides an excellent reason for being moral, namely, that one ought to be moral if one wants to avoid a dreadful punishment, and possibly gain a considerable reward as well.

The problem with this familiar viewpoint is that it confuses a purely selfish motive for being moral with the justification of morality. It makes morality a matter of prudence, which is precisely what the appeal to God as the justification of morality is intended to avoid. If morality is justified by an appeal to God, morality thereby becomes something more than an appeal to our own self-interests, namely, obedience to and love of an all-powerful, all-knowing, just, and beneficent Being. God's will defines morality not because what he commands is in our interests, but because God is the ultimate moral authority.

One final point about God and the Good. There is at least one crucial virtue in Christian theology that is sometimes elevated above morality, and that is the virtue of faith. So long as faith is one of the cardinal virtues and is understood (as Kant, for example, understood it) as directed toward morality, there is no difficulty. But if faith in God is set apart and put above morality, belief in God may not serve as a justification of morality at all. The nineteenth-century Danish philosopher Kierkegaard, for example, argues that this is the point of the Abraham and Isaac story in Genesis. Because Abraham must prove his faith in God by committing the most immoral of acts, he is forced to choose between faith and morality. The fact that God stops the sacrifice and gives the story a happy ending does not alter the fact that faith and morality can be opposed as well as conjoined.

Teleology and Human Nature

A nontheological way to introduce the notion of authority into ethics is by an appeal to nature, for example, pointing out that something serves a certain natural purpose. Thus one can say that the value of the heart in an animal is the fact that it pumps the blood around the body. This raises a further question, "What is the purpose of pumping the blood around the body?" But this too can be answered in terms of a purpose (to carry food and oxygen to the body, to eliminate waste, and so on). Eventually, we will reach an answer citing the purpose, "to keep the creature alive," at which point we may want to know whether there is some purpose to this. A practical if not very sentimental answer might be "Yes, we need pork from the pig as food in the fall." A more philosophical answer might be "Because every living thing has its place in nature." But, especially when the creature in question is one of us, we demand a sense of some further purpose, built into human nature, which, in addition to making life worth living may also provide a justification for morality.

The philosophical term for such purposive explanations and justifications is *teleology*. The word comes from the Greek word for purpose, *telos*. Aristotle, most famously, gives a teleological justification of moral virtue in his *Nicomachean Ethics*. He argues the teleological position explicitly in the well-known opening sentence of that work: "Every art and every kind of inquiry, and likewise every act and purpose, seems to aim at some good; and so it has been well said that the good is that at which everything aims." In the case of human action, Aristotle argues, this ultimate good is happiness (*eudaimonia*), the life of virtuous action in accordance with reason. How does he come to this conclusion? It is essential to human nature, he argues, to be rational. Our purpose in life, therefore, is to be as rational as possible, and being so is, if successful, happiness. Thus morality may be nothing less than obedience to our own natures, revealed to us as the moral authority of reason.

A teleological justification of morality appeals to some overriding goal built into human nature or nature in general. Aristotle takes this ultimate goal to be happiness, but this goal is part of a much larger scheme of things in which Aristotle speculates on the purpose of human existence and, ultimately, the purpose of the existence of the world. A teleological justification of morality, in other words, is a demonstration that our moral principles and virtues fit into some larger purpose.

In the preceding section, we considered the possibility that our purpose in life might be a divine purpose, an expression of God's will. Jean-Paul Sartre's response to this might be worth noting. He insists that if there is no God, there is no divine design which gives meaning to our lives. Expressing a similar view, the Russian novelist Fyodor Dostoevsky has one of his characters (Ivan Karamazov) declare, "If there is no God, everything is permitted." But the purpose of life does not have to come from God, and if there is a God, as we have seen, it does not follow that what is good is determined by him. Indeed, there is good reason to reject that view. Aristotle does not appeal to God in his theory of the function, or telos, of human life, and one can appeal to nature's purpose in support of human morality with or without reference to any divine purpose. For example, some contemporary anthropologists and sociobiologists have suggested that we are by nature a cooperative species with built-in social instincts, a view propounded by Aristotle almost twenty-five hundred years ago when he defined human beings as "social animals."

Finally, in addition to God's purpose and nature's purpose, there are our purposes. If we could show, for example that all human behavior is aimed at a single end, then that end might in turn serve as the justification of morality. Aristotle's suggestion that happiness is such an end has been repeated many times by many philosophers, throughout history. Others have suggested that pleasure is the end of all behavior. The thesis of the *hedonist*, that all our actions ultimately aim at maximizing pleasure and minimizing pain, might also serve as a justification of morality, assuming, that is, that one can show that morality does indeed lead to maximum pleasure and minimum pain. So, too, people have often argued (particularly in times of turmoil) that the ultimate purpose of human life is to live and prosper together in harmony. They say that our actions have a social purpose rather than being governed by a set of individual goals.

A different kind of ultimate purpose in life, which Aristotle conjoins with happiness, is reason. But calling reason our telos raises certain difficult questions, since reason also provides the primary basis for a very different set of theories about morality, namely, deontological theories. Immanuel Kant, for example, offers a teleological argument (much like Aristotle's) to the effect that reason is our ultimate purpose in life and therefore we ought to be rational. But Kant, as deontologist, also argues that morality is justified by appeal to reason itself, not by appeal to our purposes in life (our inclinations), such as the desire to be happy. Nevertheless, it is essential to Kant's entire philosophy that reason is our ultimate purpose in life as well as the basis of morality. (Perhaps the warning here is that one should always be wary of broad philosophical categories since the great philosophers almost always transcend them.)

Aristotle's teleological approach to ethics appeals only to human nature. It does not refer human nature to God. But after Aristotle many Christian ethicists adopted his idea that morality is a function of human reason and developed this idea in *natural law theory*. According to the theory of natural law, human rationality has been created in us by God and in the image of God, who himself is the perfectly rational being. Saint Thomas Aquinas, the greatest of the natural law theorists, equated the moral life with the life of reason, stamped in us by God, and insisted that to attack reason was equivalent to condemning God. But the difference between natural law theory and the idea that the dictates of morality are defined by God's will is all-important here. According to the view that the dictates of morality are defined by God's will, morality could be anything God might command, however unreasonable; and there is no assurance that we are rational creatures, capable of ascertaining what is right or wrong ourselves. But natural law theory does provide such assurances and, furthermore, maintains that we know the good and the right through reason, not by way of commandments from God but through the rational capacity that God gave us. Furthermore, belief in God is not a prerequisite for being moral, since God made believers and nonbelievers alike rational and capable of moral judgment. Believers realize that their reason is a gift of God, a "divine spark" within them; nonbelievers do not. They may disagree on matters of religion, but according to natural law theory they share the same God-given rational human nature and, accordingly, the same concept of morality.

Whether we are believers or unbelievers, is there any single ultimate purpose to our lives? Or, even if there is not a single purpose that is part of human nature as such, can we not justify morality by appeal to the various purposes we pursue in life? We can do so as long as we are willing to be explicit about the hypothetical nature of such justifications. For example, if we want to be respected in our own communities, we might well defend the hypothetical imperative, "If you want to be respected, then be moral and virtuous." Indeed, most of our desires in life—which is not only conducted in but made possible and meaningful by society—lend themselves to such hypothetical imperatives. Accordingly, one might argue that morality is a system of hypothetical imperatives in which each rule is conditional on some purpose or other that people pursue. While there will always be some people with purposes that dictate immorality, they are far fewer than moral cynics have sometimes suggested. Furthermore, it will be necessary for our purposes to thwart such people and their purposes. Such a qualified teleological view may therefore not provide the universal and absolute justification of morality sought by some philosophers, but it does supply a modest justification for most people. We can best get what we want out of life by being moral and virtuous. But this view need not imply that morality is just a *means* to happiness. It may also be, as Aristotle insists, an essential *part* of happiness. In other words, one of our purposes in life is to be a good person. This goal already has morality built into it, not just as a means but as an end.

Enlightened Egoism

The idea that morality can be justified by showing that it is conducive to our purposes is known as *enlightened egoism*. This theory marks a shift away from a more impersonal justification of morality by appeal to some outside authority, such as God or human nature in general, and toward a more personally oriented justification based on our aims and interests. For enlightened egoists the grounding of morality lies not in some higher good or authority but in its effectiveness in helping us to live well. But do morality and self-interest go hand in hand? Surely this is not always the case, for the dictates of morality sometimes directly conflict with our immediate interests. To resolve this conflict proponents of enlightened egoism have attempted to formulate a plausible hypothesis concerning the relationship between morality and self-interest. The following hypotheses have been offered in support of enlightened egoism.

1. *Acting morally will always lead to the satisfaction of one's own interests.*
   This assumption would make life a lot easier if it were true; we would never have to choose between what we want to do and what we ought to do. Unfortunately, life is not so simple and the thesis not very plausible.

2. *Acting morally will usually lead to the satisfaction of one's own interests.*

This thesis is certainly more plausible insofar as many of our interests include moral ambitions and are perfectly compatible with morality. It does not, however, show that one is justified in pursuing one's own self-interest in those cases in which morality and self-interest seem to conflict.

3. *Acting morally will usually, in the long run, lead to the satisfaction of more of one's interests than would be satisfied if one did not act morally.*

Not surprisingly, the more one weakens the enlightened egoist's thesis, the more plausible it becomes. Nevertheless, this point would still be a hard one to prove to a very clever villain.

4. *Acting morally will, overall, serve the greatest number of interests of the greatest number of people, including oneself.*

We are now beyond the range of egoism, enlightened or otherwise. It is one thing to claim that acting morally serves one's own interests; it is quite different to claim that acting morally serves a number of interests, including the interests of other people. This is no longer an egoistic position. It is called *utilitarianism,* and we will examine it in the following section.

5. *Acting morally will, in addition to helping to satisfy some of one's own interests, set an example which will make the world a better place in which to live.*

Thus it may satisfy other interests that have not been considered or have been given up as hopeless, such as encouraging friendliness in the streets, making everyone more cooperative and dependable, and making life generally more enjoyable. This version, unlike the others, is both egoistic and edifying. It still appeals to one's own self interest, but in such a way that it obviously has appeal to most people's shared interests and concerns as well. Moreover, this causal thesis is probably true. The world would very likely be a more satisfying place if everyone were moral and virtuous. Unfortunately, many people would have to see this happen before they agreed to cooperate, and some people would inevitably find that in a trusting, benign world the profits of immorality would be even higher and the risks considerably lower.

6. *Acting morally, whether or not it results in the satisfaction of one's own interest, inspires feelings of self-righteousness and well-being which are their own satisfactions.*

In other words, goodness is its own reward. No doubt, this is true, but what if other rewards are more attractive? Does feeling righteous alone suffice to make a person moral, or is it at best one more motive, among many others, that makes being moral more attractive? It is a common experience that self-righteousness can be extremely satisfying. But it is also a common experience that many people find certain immoral satisfactions far more attractive.

There are other formulations of enlightened egoism, but these are representative. This theory is egoism in that the focus of one's concern and the sole ground of justification is the appeal to one's own interests. It is enlightened in that it is not merely selfish but open to the suggestion that acting morally may serve one's own interests. The problem with all formulations of this theory, however, is that they tend to lose hold of the aim of a moral theory, which is to justify morality in terms of some authority apart from our purely personal interests. In other words, they tend to be prudential guidelines rather than justifications of morality as such. Morality, it is usually argued, always extends beyond the individual and his or her interests. The justification of morality, therefore, must go beyond personal interests too. What is even worse, however, is that such theories, even as prudential guidelines, tend to fail just when they are needed most, for example, when the reward for wrongdoing is huge and the threat of getting caught very small. One might well talk a petty thief out of taking a small sum by raising the prospect of going to prison, but one will hardly so influence the mobster who knows he can rake in enormous wealth with only a remote chance of being caught and convicted. So, too, it is easy to resist immoral temptation when the stakes are small, but morality outshines self-interest precisely when the stakes are highest, as in Socrates's choice of integrity over the life of a refugee.

Utilitarianism

The most influential theory of morality of the past century or so is the theory of *utilitarianism.* It is both a theory concerning the justification of morality and a formulation of the *summum bonum,* a single principle that tells us how we ought to act. It is a teleological theory, emphasizing pleasure or happiness as the desired and desirable end of all human action, but its distinction is its concern with maximizing happiness all around. The classic formulation of utilitarianism is to act so as to produce "the greatest good for the greatest number." This is what nineteenth-century utilitarian John Stuart Mill calls the utility principle. Utilitarianism insists on disinterestedness as well as self-interest; we must consider everyone's happiness and not just our own. It is a theory about what is rational as well as what is right; it tells us both how to be happy and what we ought to do. However, the theory may be limited as a distinctive theory of morality, for what might be good for the greatest number may nevertheless turn out to be immoral, and what is obviously moral may turn out not to maximize happiness.

Utilitarianism begins with the view that what motivates us is first our own happiness, but it then derives the general objective principle that we ought therefore to act not just for our own happiness but for "the greatest good for the greatest number." It is a theory that tends to put much more emphasis on results than on principles and intentions. Obedience to the utility principle is not nearly so essential to the evaluation of actions and particular rules as the consequences of those actions and rules. This has misled many people to define utilitarianism as any ethical theory that emphasizes only consequences (a definition that better fits the theory of *consequentialism*), but this focus is not its defining characteristic. Utilitarianism is essentially a teleological theory that emphasizes well-being or happiness as the ultimate end of action. It is not at all blind or indifferent to intentions or rules, but the emphasis is on beneficial and harmful results rather than on good will alone which, however well intended, may nonetheless make everyone miserable.

Utilitarianism, in one sense, goes back to the beginning of ethics (thus prompting Mill to proclaim that it has been presupposed by every moral philosopher). In the very broad sense that Mill has in mind, utilitarianism is no more than the generally acceptable and minimal view that morality requires that other people's interests must be taken into account, and everyone has an interest in being happy. But, in its more specific versions, utilitarianism is an ethical theory that promises an unusually precise means of calculating what is right and wrong. That promise is, indeed, one of the theory's main attractions. Utilitarianism, properly formulated, will not only show us how morality can be justified, but it will also show us, in detail, exactly what morality is and what, in every circumstance, we ought to do. One notion of utility assumes that there are discrete quantities of pleasure and pain which can be measured and compared. It also assumes that "each person counts for one and no more than one." In other words, everyone's pleasure (and pain) is to count equally, and it is the overall estimation of pleasure (and pain) that determines what one ought to do.

Utilitarianism had its origins in the Enlightenment, but the founder of the utilitarian movement proper was an English reformer named Jeremy Bentham who developed a "happiness calculus" to evaluate every action. For every decision, one would add up all the various pleasures it might bring to everyone concerned and subtract the amount of pain. One would compare that total with the amount resulting from alternative courses of action, and one would choose the course of action that maximized pleasure and minimized pain. Bentham's immediate aim was to reform the hopelessly complex and sometimes cruel English legal system by developing a schedule of punishments that would just outweigh the pleasures received from wrongful acts, thus minimizing the amount of pain to the smallest degree necessary to deter crime. But the theory also has application as a general ethical theory.

Suppose, for example, your elderly grandparents have asked you to come home for Thanksgiving dinner. You have an extremely important and difficult examination on the following Monday, and some of your friends, who are staying in town, are planning a great party for the Saturday night after the holiday. Your parents (who know about the exam but not the party) advise you, unhelpfully, "Do what you think best," but you know that they would like to see you with your grandparents. Now, the standard moral evaluation of this situation would raise questions such as "What is your duty in this case?" or "Do you have an obligation to your grandparents?" Not so with the utilitarian. The question is, rather, which course of action—going home or staying in town—will maximize happiness? You cannot, of course, count your own happiness as more important than that of your parents or grandparents or, though they are less involved, that of your friends. Your own happiness does count, however, and presumably that will be the first calculation. Which course of action will give you more pleasure and less pain? In the short term, studying is unpleasant (give it a minus 3) but the party will be terrific (plus 6). The trip home is a bit of a hassle (minus 2) but you do like your grandparents (plus 3). You saw your parents two weeks ago, so you don't expect any particular pleasure or pain there, but you do enjoy driving your father's new sports car (plus 2). Longer-term, if you do badly in the exam you may make it hard for yourself for years (minus 12), but if your elderly grandparents should die without your seeing them, you will also feel guilty for years (minus 12). Doing well on the exam will have considerable advantages for the future (plus 12). On the other hand, the feeling of righteousness at having pleased both your parents and your grandparents will be considerable and durable (plus 4). As for your parents, grandparents, and friends, those calculations are rather simple: your grandparents will be delighted to see you (plus 6) and your parents will too (plus 3). If they don't see you, they will be disappointed (minus 3, minus 1). Your friends (you hope) would love for you to come to the party (plus 1) but probably won't even notice if you don't (zero). The word *probably,* of course, is operative throughout your calculations, and one of the essential ingredients in Bentham's calculus is the probability of each outcome. (For our purpose here, let's assume that all of these probabilities are approximately equal.) Now, according to Bentham, we are in a position to make a completely rational decision without bringing in such obscure and unmeasurable concepts as *duty* or *obligation.* Our calculation looks like this:

Go home	*Study and go to party*
-2	-3
+3	+6
+2	-12
-12	+12
+4	-3
+6	-1
+3	+1
Totals: +4	0

The answer, clearly, is that you should go home for Thanksgiving.

In addition to the obvious difficulties and arbitrariness of quantifying people's feelings (including one's own), such calculations can involve complications. For instance, some outcomes can't be easily predicted in advance. Suppose your friends' party got out of hand. The police arrived and arrested several people (you probably would have been one of them). That, needless to say, would add considerably to the deficit side of staying in town and going to the party. Or suppose you forgot to include in the calculation the fact that you and your father have been having a continuing argument about your buying a car, which might put quite a damper on your rapport with your parents and not only cancel your sports car-driving privileges but make it much less likely that you will get a car of your own. The probabilities of such events may be small, but they nevertheless complicate the calculation and introduce a new and difficult question: To what extent must the utilitarian calculation take into account all the possible consequences of an action? To the extent we are concerned with *actual* consequences, it would seem that all consequences, no matter how unforeseen or unpredictable, count equally in the calculation of goodness and badness. To the extent that we are concerned just with *envisioned* consequences, on the other hand, we will include only what a responsible person could reasonably expect to happen. One must also add into the calculus the effort, pleasure, and pain that go into the calculation itself. For example, if you spend the two weeks before Thanksgiving worrying about what to do, not studying, and being irritable with your friends and on the phone with your parents, you may well cause yourself and everyone else sufficient pain to cancel out all the expected benefits of either course of action. Indeed, in many ordinary decisions in life, trying too hard to make a precisely rational decision is itself quite irrational.

Now it may have struck you that this attempt at rational decision-making ultimately seems rather pointless. Pleasures and pains are difficult to measure and the numerical amounts assigned may seem arbitrary. It is not always easy to assess how much you will enjoy yourself or suffer, much less assess someone else's pleasure and pain. But most disturbing of all is the fact that this utilitarian accounting system seems to treat all pleasures and pains on a par, as if there were no difference between them except in their amounts. Bentham himself insisted "Pushpin [a mindless game of the time] is as good as poetry." Thus utilitarianism acquired an unflattering reputation for being vulgar and without standards.

The ultimate champion of utilitarianism would not be Bentham but John Stuart Mill, the son of Bentham's colleague James Mill. In his definitive pamphlet *Utilitarianism* (1861), Mill defends the principle of utility as the only intelligible basis for ethics, but at the same time he amends Bentham's calculus with a conception of the quality of pleasure. If one gets much more pleasure in drinking beer than reading Shakespeare, Mill does not want to be forced to conclude that the first act is better than the second. Thus he writes, "It is better to be a Socrates dissatisfied, than a pig satisfied." This amendment all but destroyed the simplicity of Bentham's calculus, for it was the ability to calculate all ethical decisions on a single scale of pleasure and pain that made the utilitarian program so appealing to those who wanted straightforward moral solutions. But once one has shifted the argument away from measurable quantities of pleasure and pain (even assuming that these are available), how does one evaluate their qualities? We have lost our calculus, and it is by no means clear that a more complicated qualitative calculus can take its place.

Contemporary theorists have distinguished a surprisingly large number of utilitarian theories, all of them tied to the "greatest good for the greatest number" idea. For example, utilitarianism is sometimes interpreted as a retrospective way of evaluating the actual consequences of actions. Sometimes it is interpreted as a technique for planning actions, for evaluating intentions rather than consequences, assuming, of course, that intentions also take into account probable consequences. Mill's theorizing incorporates both these views; he would say that the first approach is a means of evaluating actions and the second a means of evaluating personal character. Utilitarians are also split on whether or not to accept Mill's and Bentham's equation of happiness with pleasure. Like Aristotle, many utilitarians want to separate the two and insist that it is happiness that is important, not pleasure as such (though obviously one wouldn't want to suggest that the two are completely opposed). But happiness, as we have seen, is a broad and equivocal concept, while the notions of pleasure and pain seem more precise. More orthodox utilitarians have continued the emphasis on quantifiable (if not qualifiable) pleasure as a way of saving the utility of utilitarianism. Other thinkers have rejected both pleasure and happiness and have focused instead on the notion of preferences. Satisfying people's preferences, whether or not these provide pleasure or maximize happiness, is an adequate criterion of utility. What remains constant in all versions of utilitarianism, of course, is the emphasis on desirable consequences, the greatest good for the greatest number. But despite its apparent simplicity, utilitarianism is not a single theory but many, with very different emphases and many different evaluations of consequences.

Perhaps the most important division among utilitarians today turns on a question we have not yet broached, namely, Is it an individual action to which we apply the utilitarian calculus, or is it, rather, a class of actions? Suppose, for example, I am tempted to tell a lie. This is, of course, one of the standard moral dilemmas, in which the principle of utility is typically thought to be inappropriate. We tend to think, It doesn't matter that everyone will be happier if you lie; it's wrong to tell a lie! It is easy to imagine an instance in which the happy consequences of a lie overwhelm the few painful consequences, including the modicum of shame or guilt and the small effort necessary for the cover-up. Furthermore, the consequences of telling the truth may be devastating for the person to whom the upsetting truth is told and, consequently, extremely unpleasant for the truth-teller too. Looking only at this individual act, the utilitarian decision is obvious. One ought to lie, thereby maximizing happiness and minimizing suffering. But, a critic might well contend, it is never an isolated action that is the subject of our deliberations and our ethics. To call an act a lie is already to place it in a class of actions that are morally dubious. When we evaluate the consequences of lying, therefore, it is not just a question of whether this lie has good or bad consequences for everyone involved. It is a question of whether lying as such has good or bad consequences.

This point changes our view of the matter considerably, needless to say. An individual act of lying may well have obviously good consequences, but it is not at all clear that lying in general has anything but bad consequences. Lying makes both liars and those lied to unhappy in a myriad of ways, and the "white lie" is something of an exception. Thus we can distinguish two distinct forms of utilitarianism (both of which, by the way, seem to be contained in Mill's *Utilitarianism*):

1. Always do that act which will bring the greatest good to the greatest number (*act-utilitarianism*).
2. Always do that kind of act (or follow that rule) which will bring the greatest good to the greatest number (*rule-utilitarianism*).

Why have utilitarians split on this seemingly technical issue? (Mill, by contrast, seems content to consider the general implications of an action as part of its consequences; implicit support for a rule or a class of actions is one of the considerations in deciding the utilitarian quality of an act.) The reason is that as act-utilitarianism has been increasingly challenged by difficult cases, rule-utilitarianism has provided a way to save utilitarianism in general from the most troublesome objections. For example, the objection has often been raised that a proper calculation of the consequences of an action is humanly impossible (thus our concern for unforeseen consequences and the difficulty of predicting people's feelings in our Thanksgiving example). But in rule-utilitarianism one need not undertake such individual calculations, for they have already been provided in the general form of a rule. Thus, "Lying is wrong" is a summary statement of centuries of research and observation showing that lying in general leads to bad consequences.

A second much-noted difficulty with act-utilitarianism can be summarized in the following example. Suppose you were to carry out the utilitarian calculations appropriate to two courses of action, one of which includes both a lie and a clearly unfair action in which another person will be cheated. Consider, for example, selling a used car using the claim that it is in excellent running condition even though you know that it will fall apart in five miles. Suppose, too, that the balance of utility in your calculation comes out even. The person buying the car is quite rich and has several other cars, while you desperately need the money and have to leave town to visit your sickly old uncle. On a strict act-utilitarian basis, the choice between telling the truth and lying is indifferent.

Not surprisingly, such a conclusion would not be acceptable to most people. The choice to lie and cheat or not to should never be a matter of indifference. One could, as a convinced act-utilitarian, dig in one's heels and insist that such moral concerns are indeed irrelevant. But most utilitarians regard such examples as more than sufficient to damage the act-utilitarian theory, and they prefer to modify utilitarianism to get around them. Rule-utilitarianism is the best known of these modifications.

The various forms of utilitarianism, all of them originating in the simple, appealing principle of utility formulated by Bentham and Mill, reflect the problems in the theory. Each variation is an attempt to modify the theory to answer an objection. Indeed, the strength and influence of utilitarianism are exemplified by the number of serious revisions of it. Less compelling theories are usually just left to wither away. The first variation of the theory was Mill's objection to Bentham's purely quantitative theory, which placed too much emphasis on material pleasures and not enough on the harder-to-quantify pleasures of the mind and spirit, such as the arts, friendship, and philosophy. A more recent variation of utilitarian theory is the formulation of rule utilitarianism, as a way of meeting the objection that clearly wrong acts might in a single instance be shown to maximize pleasure and minimize pain for everyone involved. Rule-utilitarianism blocks this possibility by insisting that a class of actions, not just a single instance, improves the general well-being. It also accounts for the value of moral rules.

Utilitarianism continues to be one of the most thoroughly discussed ethical theories and strategies of moral justification, but it is not without its continuing problems. As a theory of utility it has always been accused of being vulgar and devoid of more spiritual awareness, despite Mill's efforts to add quality to it. Indeed, Mill counters this objection in *Utilitarianism,* when he answers religious critics who attack him for linking morality to a businesslike calculation of pleasures instead of to God or the Scriptures. Mill's reply is simply that God, being good, wants us to be happy, and so God himself is a utilitarian and utilitarianism is just a precise way of interpreting God's will.

A more telling set of objections is aimed at the utilitarian emphasis on consequences, whether of an action or a class of actions, whether the consequences are actual or intended. When a moral principle is presented absolutely, as in the Ten Commandments, for example, the question of consequences need not arise, or arises only secondarily. (Moses did not ask Jehovah, "So what would happen if people started to covet their neighbors' oxen?") Such rules may admit of qualifications and exceptions, but their status as rules comes first. We may object to this emphasis on rules, and we may use utilitarianism (even rule-utilitarianism) against it. But to insist that consequences are important or even essential to morality is not to deny that rules may be important too, and that they may override considerations of the general good. Consider, for instance, one of the most common counterexamples to the utilitarian theory, the sadist or the sick society that gets great joy out of the spectacle of a few innocent people being tortured to death, such as Roman society during some of its darker days. On the utilitarian account, the great joy of the spectators, if it outweighs the suffering of the few victims, is sufficient to make their behavior moral. Indeed, given a sufficiently large component of sadism in a population, this means of maximizing pleasure, if not minimizing pain, might be promoted as a national sport. But this, we object, would surely be unfair and immoral. The example suggests that utilitarianism cannot take proper account of justice. The well-being of the majority is one thing, but justice is another matter. Happily, the two are usually commensurate. But, nevertheless, as an overall theory of the justification of morality, utilitarianism has been accused of failing a crucial test. It cannot provide adequate justification for some of our most important moral convictions.

So, too, utilitarianism seems to presume that different kinds of consequences can be readily compared. Throughout our discussion we have assumed the intelligibility of Bentham's first premise, that different units of utility (whether pleasure and pain, happiness and unhappiness, or good and evil) can be placed on a similar scale and weighed. Mill is suspicious of this, which is why he introduces the notion of quality of pleasure, allowing for different scales of measurement but thereby destroying the simplicity and singularity of Bentham's calculus. But can we really compare different values on any single set of scales? Suppose a city is in a financial crisis and one of the suggestions for saving money is closing down the art museum and selling its contents. Closing down the museum may save the taxpayers thousands of dollars, but what is the cultural cost of doing so? When the less tangible aspects of human life are involved, we are rightfully squeamish about trying to put a concrete value on them. There is something ethically discomforting about life insurance, the art market, and commercialized religion because the value of life or a work of art or a religious belief does not seem reducible to any ordinary measurement. So, too, our moral values do not seem to be appropriate for ordinary bargaining and comparison with personal pleasures and preferences, and they cannot be supported simply by appealing to the principle of the greatest good for the greatest number. Suppose, for example, it could be demonstrated that adultery would save more marriages than it would destroy and would make people more happy than miserable. Would adultery then be a moral act? Such research has often been attempted, but the results have generally been rejected, not because of lack of evidence, but because such results violate our sense of morality. If adultery is wrong, as most people still believe, it does not matter whether it is conducive to happiness or not.

All of these objections have been answered by various utilitarians, of course, but, despite utilitarian arguments and improvements, many philosophers have been persuaded to look elsewhere for the nature and justification of morality.

Kant and Deontology

In reaction to the objections raised against utilitarianism a great many philosophers have turned to an older tradition in which moral principles are not conditional on consequences or merely the means to happiness, but are absolute. The origins of this tradition may go back to the beginning of human history, when the command of the chief, or the king, or God, was given unconditionally. One had an obligation to obey authority regardless of the consequences. Whereas utilitarian theories ground morality in the pursuit of human happiness, theories based on moral absolutes ground morality in the concept of obligation. We noted earlier that the word deontological comes from the Greek root *deon,* meaning "duty." In deontological theories an act or a class of actions is justified by showing that it is right, not by showing that it has good consequences (though, again, it is usually assumed that right action will have good consequences). But unlike the unconditional and unquestioning obedience of ancient tribes to a ruler's or to God's commands, the notion of right involved in deontological theories is not imposed or determined by any chief or king or divine being. Rather, obligations one feels are self-imposed. The all-important concept in deontological theories, accordingly, is *autonomy,* thinking and acting for oneself and doing what one knows is right.

The foremost modern defender of a deontological theory of morality was Immanuel Kant. He was reacting to the early utility theories of David Hume and other Enlightenment philosophers, and he anticipated the later objections to utilitarianism. (Kant wrote seventy years before

Mill.) Kant insists that what makes an act right or wrong is not its consequences, which are often entirely out of our hands or a matter of luck, but rather the principle, or *maxim,* that guides the action. "Nothing . . . can be called good without qualification, except a *good will*," he writes at the beginning of his *Grounding of the Metaphysic of Morals.* And having a good will means acting with the right intentions, according to the right maxims or principles, doing one's duty for its own sake rather than for personal gain or out of what Kant calls "inclination" (desire, emotion, mood, whim, inspiration, or sympathy). This is the heart of Kant's ethics—duty for duty's sake, not for the sake of the consequences, whether one's own good or the greatest good for the greatest number.

What is the ground of appeal for deontological theories? The utilitarian, like the enlightened egoist and the Aristotelean teleologist, could appeal to actual human desires and aspirations. But the deontologist, requiring an unconditional or absolute reference point, rejects those desires and aspirations as the ultimate grounds for moral behavior, though for Kant and almost all other deontologists they nevertheless remain important. The ground of appeal for a deontological theory is reason. Kant calls it "pure practical reason." Each of us is rational; that is, each of us has the ability to reason and arrive at the *right* way to act by ourselves and without appeal to any outside authority. Each of us can figure out for ourselves what it is that we ought to do and not do. The authority necessary to justify morality is one's own moral autonomy. To justify morality, therefore, is to show that it is rational, and to justify any particular moral principle is to show that it is in accordance with the principles of reason. Morality, as we indicated in part 1 is characterized by Kant as a system of categorical imperatives, that is, commands that are unconditional. We can now appreciate better what this means; the commands are unconditional not only in the sense that they apply to everyone without referring to personal interests but also in the sense that they are principles of reason and, as such, are not bound to the contingencies of life. They apply without regard to consequences. Kant takes this to be the heart of reason, that it envisions the world according to its own ideals and is not determined merely by the facts of the world.

Because moral principles are rational principles, according to Kant, their test must be purely *formal*. To prove that an act is immoral, it is not enough to show that its actual or probable consequences would be disastrous. One must demonstrate that the underlying principle itself is contradictory and impossible. One of Kant's examples will serve as an illustration of what this means. Suppose I am considering borrowing money from you under false pretenses, by lying and telling you that I will pay you back next week (when in fact I will already be in Hawaii, never to return). The utilitarian would calculate the consequences (whether of the act or of the kind of act), but Kant insists that the act is wrong no matter what the consequences. What if, he argues, I were to apply the maxim of my act (that is, the principle upon which I am acting) to everyone else, and urge them to act similarly? Since morality is essentially a product of reason, I must be able to do this, for I cannot apply principles to myself alone. (The utilitarian would agree with this.) What would be the result? It would be to undercut the whole practice of promising to repay borrowed money, and if anyone were to ask, "Can I borrow some money and pay you back next week?" everyone would simply laugh because such words would have become meaningless. Thus, Kant insists, the maxim contradicts itself in the sense that it could not be universalized as a principle of action for everyone without undermining the very possibility of performing such an action. This is not just to say that the consequences of generalizing the maxim would be disastrous. (A rule-utilitarian would agree with that.) It is a formal or logical inadequacy: the universalization of the maxim makes the action in question incomprehensible. For what would count as lying in a community in which no one could ever be expected to tell the truth?

Notice that Kant's philosophy does not deny any reference or appeal to the consequences of an action. He makes no appeal to the actual consequences of an action—for who could know these before the action is carried out?—but he does include the intended consequences of the action in his formulation of the maxim itself. He also makes reference to the imagined consequences of the act or maxim universalized, so it would not be correct to say (although it is often said) that Kant rejects *any* appeal to consequences. But in comparison to the utilitarian's direct and often exclusive concern with consequences, Kant's ethics surely provides a distinct contrast.

Part of what motivates Kant's deontology is a firm conviction that morality is something more than the customs and ethos of a particular society, something more than a set of sympathetic feelings we experience toward other people and other creatures. He believes, and wants to prove, that morality must be the same everywhere, built into the structure of the human mind just as the basic categories of truth and knowledge are. This does not mean that everyone everywhere in fact accepts all the same moral principles. (Neither do all people accept the principles of modern science, which Kant also insists are universal and necessarily true "for every rational being.") His argument is that every human being has the faculty of rationality, though not every human being actually cultivates and realizes that faculty. In effect, what Kant wants to do with his philosophy, as Aristotle wanted to do with his, is to help people cultivate their rational faculty by understanding better what it means to be moral and consequently becoming more moral. But he will readily admit that most people and most of the peoples of the world fall far short of his rational ideal.

The crucial point in Kant's approach is that it is not just our personal inclinations that motivate us to act. There is a far nobler source of motivation, and that is reason itself. In other words, Kant thinks that egoism, enlightened or otherwise, is just plain false. We are not motivated only by self-interest. We are also motivated to act for the sake of reason alone. Thus the recognition that we have a duty need not be further supported by some realization of self-interest; it is enough that we recognize our duty, and because we are rational, we want to do it. This statement also embodies the central notion of autonomy in Kant's philosophy. Not only can we think for ourselves and figure out what is right and wrong; we can also act contrary to our inclinations, including our most powerful desires and emotions, if they do not conform to the dictates of practical reason. This sense of autonomous moral motivation, animated not by sympathy or any other inclination but by "the moral law within" makes Kant's ethics the most powerful defense of pure morality in the history of the subject.

This emphasis on the moral law within and the notion of autonomy is at odds with the grounding of morality in utility or any other social concept. For Kant, morality is essentially an individual as well as a universal affair. It is individual in that, as an autonomous subject, each person has both the ability and the duty to reason and figure out what is right. It is universal in that, because each of us is rational, the laws of reason and the principles of morality dictated by reason are necessary and shared by all of us. But what is left out of this notion of autonomy is the social fabric of an ethos, the sense of our being social animals, as Aristotle defined us so long ago. Kant does not lack a keen sense of community and he clearly sees the need for all of us to get along. Indeed, one of his formulations of the categorical imperative is that we should always act as if we were members of the perfect community, which he calls "the kingdom of ends." But it is doing our duty itself that is essential to morality. The good society, one hopes, will follow. Kant is well aware that societies as well as individuals can be immoral. Morals, therefore, cannot consist of the values and relationships within a society. Reason transcends all societies and dictates a set of rational principles which are to be obeyed by all.

Deontological theories such as Kant's succeed precisely where utilitarian theories fail, in showing how moral principles are unconditional and not dependent on utility, especially in those cases where the greatest good for the greatest number can be realized through injustice or cruelty. Where the deontologist runs into trouble, however, is just where the utilitarian succeeds. One of the great attractions of utilitarianism is its emphasis on human happiness and well-being. The deontologist is not indifferent to such concerns, but they clearly play a secondary role in the theory of morality. Morality must be independent of personal inclinations (including the desire to be happy) for the inclinations are variable and undependable rather than necessary and universal. And, in contrast to Kant's notion of autonomy, the inclinations are not subject to a free and rational will. But is it possible or tolerable that happiness should be opposed to morality? To be sure, there are occasions in which we are obliged to do what we do not want to do. But could this opposition be general and imply an antagonism between doing right and living well?

This intolerable conclusion is precisely what utilitarianism, and enlightened egoism, deny. But Kant also rejects this conclusion, insisting that we even have a duty to be happy. His odd reason is that an unhappy person is not in an optimum mood to carry out his or her duties. Furthermore, he says, rationality dictates that it would be most unreasonable to expect us to do our duty if there were no justice, no reward of happiness for goodness, no punishment for evil. But since it is obvious that we do not always find justice in this world, Kant argues that its absence should rationally lead us to conclude that there must be justice elsewhere, in an afterlife judged by an all-knowing and all-powerful beneficent God. Thus Kant, like many deontologists before him, ultimately ties his strict sense of morality and duty to religion, albeit a rational religion, one that can be defended "through reason alone." But notice that Kant places religious belief on a moral foundation. He does not justify morality on the authority of God but rather grounds both morality and religion in the authority of autonomous reason.

Existentialism, Emotivism, and Moore: Why Justification?

In the preceding sections we have discussed two general types of ethical theory: teleological theories which appeal to the ultimate purposes and consequences of moral behavior, and deontological theories which appeal to the rational authority of moral principles. We have also considered a number of particular grounds of appeal, among them God's will, practical reason, the formal consistency of principles, and natural human desires and aspirations, including selfishness as well as more enlightened egoism. For more than two thousand years, debate has raged over these strategies and the ultimate validity of such appeals, and ethicists will probably continue debating their various advantages and inadequacies for the next two thousand years as well. But there is another possibility, and that is that the entire enterprise of justifying morality and theorizing about its foundation is a mistake. Perhaps morality cannot be justified, or perhaps the attempt to justify morality already indicates some deep insecurity about morality, such that we are not convinced of its necessity without some proof or demonstration.

This insecurity can be detected even in the staunchest defenders of morality. Some of the sophists who converse with Socrates in Plato's dialogues, offer persuasive arguments against morality—that might makes right, that justice is nothing but timid selfishness, that man is the measure of all things—and it is not entirely clear that Socrates refutes them. Aristotle warns us at the beginning of his *Ethics* that we should not expect more precision or proof than the subject allows and insists that there is no point in trying to convince people of the importance of the virtues if they have not already been brought up correctly to accept and practice them. Mill prefaces his "proof" of utilitarianism with the similar warning that one cannot really prove ultimate principles in ethics. Sometimes, however, the insecurity develops into full-scale skepticism, as in the work of David Hume and Friedrich Nietzsche.

Hume rejects the possibility of justifying morals (just as he rejects the possibility of justifying our knowledge of the world) because he thinks that there are no sound arguments with factual premises that will yield moral judgments as their conclusion. Like many philosophers, Hume distinguishes sharply between facts and values, between *is* and *ought* statements. How is it, Hume asks, that we feel justified in reasoning from some fact or facts about the world, that doing a certain thing feels good or makes us happy, to the judgment that one ought to do that thing? All such inferences, Hume suggests, are invalid. Morals, he insists, are based on our sentiments, not reason. The fact that we are naturally sympathetic does not mean that we ought to be so, however, and thus hardly counts as a justification of morality in the strong sense demanded by philosophers. After all, if our sentiments were entirely different, so would be our morals. The question of which morals are right thus seems beside the point. It just happens that we are endowed by nature with certain sentiments (as it happens that we are endowed by nature with certain facilities for knowledge), and that's the end of it. Reason alone, Hume argues, can neither motivate nor justify our behavior. And yet Hume himself was a morally conservative citizen and did not advocate immorality. There is no justification for morality, he maintains, but neither is one needed.

Nietzsche, however, does not stop there. He argues that not only is there is no justification for morality but there are some very good arguments against it. Nietzsche asks why there should be so much emphasis on justification, if it is not because morality itself has lost its persuasiveness and we no longer believe in it. Traditional morality depends on the belief in God, Nietzsche surmises, and if people no longer believe in God as a moral force, then wouldn't they also lose faith in the moral world order, perhaps without admitting it to themselves? Why the insistence on reason, he asks, if it is not because we fear our natural passions and aspirations, as if we need formal principles to keep our spirits in check. And why, he asks, this emphasis on universal principles, if not in order to impose the same set of restricting demands and expectations on everyone, thus stunting the growth of those few who could excel far beyond the others? Could history have produced a Caesar or a Napoleon, or for that matter a Michelangelo, if such figures had restricted themselves to everyday morals? Morality, Nietzsche concludes, is not justifiable, not because philosophers haven't come up with a wholly acceptable justification, but because there is something seriously wrong with the very idea of morality. Morality, Nietzsche argues, is a reactionary value system that rejects the virtues of strength and creativity and replaces them with such dubious virtues as meekness, humility, and innocence. The commands of morality are really a covert strategy for the protection of the weak. Morality, Nietzsche maintains, is not the noble aspect of our lives that we have pretended; rather, it is a hypocritical expression of weakness.

An equally radical theory is expounded by the French existentialist Jean-Paul Sartre. He rejects the attempt to justify morality on the grounds that any such justification only shifts the ultimate responsibility for what we do away from our own free choice. Suppose a young man has to choose between joining the army to fight for his country or staying home with his grieving mother, who has already lost her husband and two sons in the war. What is the principle he should follow in making his decision? The fact is, Sartre argues, that he has to make a decision, and in doing so, he might endorse a number of principles (such as that one's primary obligation is to one's mother), but both the decision and its justification are nothing other than his having made his choice and having to live with it. We can see that Sartre takes Kant's insistence on individual autonomy to its extreme. Not only must we choose among alternatives and can we make a choice contrary to even our strongest inclinations, we are also responsible for determining what it is that is to count as right and wrong. The problem is thus one of choosing to live in "good faith," which means, among other things, not falsely appealing to any authority, including reason, to support one's own free choices.

As flamboyant and passionate as the statements of Nietzsche and the existentialists are, the rejection of the whole program of justifying morality has had its most radical and influential expression in the sober academic pronouncements of English and American analytic philosophers of this century. The pivotal figure in this development was the Cambridge philosopher G. E. Moore, who shook up an entire tradition in ethics with his *open question argument.* The open question argument begins with a sharp distinction, as in Hume, between facts and values and then argues that value claims cannot be proven by any number of facts. One can always ask the open question, "Yes, but is it good?" Moore's own response to this question was that *good* is the name of a "simple, undefinable, non-natural property" which we know by intuition, thus giving rise to a theory called *intuitionism.* One knows that something is good by simply "seeing that it is so" but cannot prove it is good by appealing to the facts or to any abstract principle of reason. Moore argued that one cannot justify morality in the usual sense; that is, one cannot prove it by appeal to reason or purposes or consequences, but nevertheless one can know what is good. On that basis Moore defended a version of utilitarianism. What he rejected was the traditional proof of utilitarianism, exemplified by Mill, in which good is identified with some natural property or widespread desire such as pleasure or prosperity.

Moore's followers were not so optimistic about their ability to intuit the good. They accepted his open question argument but rejected his intuitionism and utilitarianism. Some of them concluded that morality and ethics in general (as well as religion, aesthetics, and any number of other nonempirical disciplines) are devoid of substantial cognitive content. Attempting to justify them makes no more sense than trying to justify your preference for chocolate fudge ice cream. The leading movement in this wholesale rejection of ethics was called *logical positivism,* which had its origin among a number of German and Austrian philosophers and scientists who fled the Nazis in the 1930s. Their view of ethics was that opinions about values are mainly matters of emotion, not knowledge. The ethical theory developed by some of the logical positivists, notably by A. J. Ayer in England and C. L. Stevenson in the United States, was accordingly called *emotivism*. They argued, following Hume, that value judgments cannot be based wholly on facts and that statements in ethics, therefore, are not matters of knowledge and cannot be justified as matters of fact. Thus, the general position of a great many contemporary philosophers has come to be called *noncognitivism*, which means that ethical statements are neither true nor false and cannot be known or justified as such.

Noncognitivism has had several variants in England and the United States in the past fifty years. Emotivism—the very strong noncognitivist view that making a moral judgment is logically on a par with yelling "Hooray" (A. J. Ayer's formulation)—was popular for a decade or so, but it ran up against a powerful objection, namely, it left little room for an adequate account of moral reasoning, or how we deliberate and persuade ourselves and others of the rightness or wrongness of an action. Such an account is essential to ethics, for, as we have seen, moral judgments consist not just of personal passions and preferences but of claims that at least purport to have rational, disinterested, objective status. To be sure, one can provoke emotion in other people through argument and one can persuade people through a variety of rhetorical devices, but the idea of justification is rejected by emotivism and with it the claim that moral views are correct or incorrect. Ideally, such radical relativism might eliminate a good many moral disagreements, but it also eliminates the very moral judgment that motivated the logical positivists in the first place. If moral judgments are no more than expressions of emotion, then how does one argue with a fanatic, a Nazi, whose passions may be profound but whose opinions are immoral and intolerable? Whether or not morality is mainly a matter of reason, moral judgments require reasons. Noncognitivism, accordingly, gave up emotivism and shifted its attention back to the reasons we give to back up our moral claims.

Some undergraduates adopt a version of emotivism when they claim that all value judgments are subjective and dismiss any moral claim as "just a value judgment." But the difference between the noncognitivist and the undergraduate subjectivist positions is significant. The logical positivists and other noncognitivists developed elaborate theories of language and knowledge in support of their claim that ethics is not a matter of knowledge. The undergraduate subjectivist all too often uses only the glib conclusion and dispenses with the arguments and theories. The logical positivists defended their noncognitivism in order to root out much nonsense from the realm of moral discussion. Too many undergraduate subjectivists adopt the noncognitivist position as a way of avoiding criticism or worse, to avoid thinking about ethics at all. But, as many noncognitivists are now arguing, ethical claims nevertheless have their reasons, and ethics, even if subjective, nevertheless requires some objectively valid reasoning.

The Justification of Morality and the Problem of Relativism

Why are philosophers so concerned with the justification of morality? In part, they are concerned to know that what we do is right, and that we are justified in encouraging or forcing others, such as our children, immigrants, rebels, and deviants, to conform to certain ways of behaving. With many social customs, we may be content merely to insist that that's the way we do things here. We are perfectly willing to accept that people elsewhere do things differently. But where morality is concerned, as in issues such as sexual behavior and the treatment of children, we are not willing simply to accept such differences. The justification of morality is thus an attack on *ethical relativism,* the view that different people have different moral systems and that no position is more correct than any other.

The theories we have looked at thus far deny relativism in various ways. Kant asserts that morality consists of absolute, unconditional principles, and the utilitarians insist that all moralities may be judged by a single, universal standard, namely, the extent to which they do, or do not, maximize general happiness. The Judeo-Christian tradition eliminates the problem of relativism with the doctrine of one God and a single set of moral laws for all people. Plato and Aristotle, while recognizing the differences between their own values and the values of other cultures and classes, simply assumed that the values of Athenian aristocrats were superior to all others and saw no need to prove the point.

Throughout most of the history of ethics, ethical relativism was at best an eccentric thesis, defended on occasion by a few skeptics and some of the German romantics who were fighting against the moral imperialism of the English and the French during the eighteenth and nineteenth century. (Kant was obviously not one of them.) But today, at the end of the twentieth century, ethical relativism, like relativity in physics, is an inescapable thesis. With air travel and telecommunications now commonplace, the world has gotten much smaller. Communities and cultures that were far apart in space and consequently in time are now neighbors, elbow to elbow, and the clash of differing mores and morals is commonplace. We are a multicultural society in which the differences between us are often more pronounced than the similarities. The idea that what is right might vary from culture to culture and community to community can be seen as both an attractive and repulsive thesis. On the positive side, relativism can encourage acceptance of differences and reduce friction. On the negative side, it can aggravate disagreements and increase hostility. In ethics, our task is to understand what relativism claims and entails, and what it does not claim and entail. Is relativism a plausible thesis?

Some thinkers have argued that if we were to accept relativism ethics in general and morality in particular would be undermined. If "it's all relative," then what is the point of arguing for one moral position rather than another, unless it is for the practical purpose of winning someone to your side. But the idea that there might be a number of different but equally correct moralities has often struck philosophers as a contradiction in terms. Either an act is moral, or it is not. The idea that an act could be moral in France and immoral in Japan must rest on some basic confusion. Either the act is *believed* to be moral in one place but not in the other, in which case at least one culture is wrong, or the difference is being misdescribed. Moral philosophers argue, for example, that although the superficial aspects of morals may differ from society to society, the deep structures of morals—for example, some version of respect and human dignity or the pursuit of happiness—are the same the world over. Thus a comment or gesture might be a routine daily wisecrack in Paris but a sign of disrespect in Tokyo. The first act would be moral (or at least, not immoral) and the second would be highly offensive and immoral. But in a deeper sense the two acts are being judged according to the same shared value of respect for others. It is just that what counts as respect is different in France and in Japan. Relativism, by this account, describes superficial differences between societies. It does not present a threat to morality or make moral disagreements in principle unresolvable.

Some philosophers have argued that ethical relativism is, on the face of it, an absurd or self-refuting thesis. They claim that it is absurd or meaningless to say, "This is morally good in society X but not in society Y," just as it would be meaningless to say that a factual claim in science is true for one society (e.g., pre-Copernican Europe) and false for another (e.g., the post-Einsteinian scientific world). Either something is true or it is not. Either something is morally good or it is not. If we drop the word *morally,* of course, it makes sense to say that something is good for people in one society and not for another. A hot fire at night is good in northern Alaska but not so good in Cameroon. But to say that something is a moral issue seems to entail that there is a right or wrong choice of action regardless of context. Thus we have (tentatively) followed Kant in his insistence that morality is universal. When we say that something is immoral, we seem to be saying that it is wrong, not just that we don't like it or don't approve of it. It might make sense to say that something is *considered* morally good in society X but not in society Y, but again the implication is that either society is wrong or there is some basic, shared moral consideration that explains the difference.

Ethical relativism is often confused with cultural relativism, on which it is loosely based. *Cultural relativism* is a descriptive thesis based on anthropological observation: different cultures do indeed have different ideas about what is right and wrong. *Ethical relativism,* on the other hand, is the view that what is right is relative to different cultures. The denial that there are any deep differences in moral matters among cultures is part of the cultural relativity debate. But on the basis of anthropological observation of the past several centuries it must be said that this denial is almost certainly false (though this demonstration is in the domain of empirical social science, not in that of ethics). Let us simply assume here that deep moral differences among cultures are an established fact. Not only do people get married in different ways and under different conditions; the very concepts of marriage and family are decidedly different in different cultures. Not only does what counts as stealing vary from culture to culture; the very notion of stealing is absent in some, extremely important in others. But if these differences are true, does cultural relativism entail ethical relativism?

The answer, again, is no. One might well accept differences in various peoples' ideas of right and wrong and yet insist, as Kant did, that some of those ideas are just plain wrong. There is no paradox or self-contradiction here. Cultural relativism does not entail ethical relativism.

Indeed, the visibility of the former may only reinforce a moralist's disdain for the latter. Ethical relativism is itself an ethical thesis. It insists that we not only recognize moral differences but respect them too. But notice there is a contradiction in asserting as a universal principle that everyone everywhere ought to respect ethical differences. The ethical relativist is asserting as a universally correct principle that there are no universally correct principles. Moreover, not everyone agrees with the principle of tolerance that many relativists espouse. Of course, almost everyone is willing to tolerate slight differences, but when it becomes a disagreement over matters that are sacred or otherwise central to a culture's view of the good, tolerance quickly gives way to condemnation. How, then, should the ethical relativist deal with such disagreements? When the principle of tolerance is itself in dispute, it doesn't make much sense to limply say, "Oh, well, we simply disagree about that, but you're just as right as I am and I respect your opinion." On the other hand, it is no less paradoxical or absurd for the ethical relativist to insist adamantly that a particular view is wrong. According to whom? According to the relativist's relative standards? Certainly not according to the opponent's own standards.

The problem for the relativist is where to stand while pronouncing the doctrine that one moral view is as correct or incorrect as another. If he or she is living inside a particular culture, then there are surely some moral claims one can make, in which case the doctrine would certainly be rejected. It may well be that killing one's grandparents by leaving them out on the ice is morally permissible and explicable in certain Eskimo cultures. And though one might be tolerant and argue that geriatricide is right in certain cultures in certain circumstances, this admission does not in any sense weaken one's own belief that it is wrong to kill one's grandparents. If the relativist steps outside his or her culture, he or she may say something like, "Geriatricide is considered moral in certain cultures but not in America," but this in no way suggests that one morality is as good as another. The relativist has already stepped out of the moral context in which such comparisons are possible.

To accept cultural relativism and to be an ethical relativist does not mean that one cannot compare moral systems, evaluate them, and choose between them. It certainly does not mean, as too many people take it to mean, that any culture and any ethics is as good as any other culture or any other ethics. In many cases, two systems include principles in common which can be employed to judge one course of action as morally better than another. If we disagree with the Australians about their treatment of aborigines, this is not a matter of ethical relativism. The Australians have the same principles of equality and fairness that Americans do; the dispute is one of politics and historical circumstances rather than a disagreement about basic moral values. If some ultimate good or purpose is shared by two cultures, that good or purpose may also be used to judge one moral system as better or worse. For example, if a communist culture and a capitalist culture (assuming that these are moral as well as economic systems) agreed that the ultimate purpose of each culture is to make its citizens happy and materially comfortable, then there would be no question of ethical relativism, just the straightforward question about which system in fact makes people happier and more comfortable.

The real problem begins when ultimate principles and purposes clash. We need not go to the islands and jungles explored by anthropologists to see such a problem in progress, however. Consider the abortion issue in the United States. Even without bringing in the religious dimension of the dispute, it is clear that the ultimate principles, "right to life" and "individual choice," are in direct confrontation, even if both parties accept both principles and disagree only on their priority. But this often violent dispute can show us quite clearly which versions of ethical relativism make sense and which do not. A person who is not very involved in the argument can observe and listen to both sides and conclude that they both have a point. The observer may even get involved and choose a side, pursuing one line of argument but not the other. But what the observer cannot say, except ironically, is that they are both right. Nor is it valid to conclude, because both sides are supported by powerful principles and strong arguments, that one morality is as correct as another. So what is the relativist to say?

Disagreements in ethics are frequently very intense and difficult, and if there is no general agreement about basic principles and their priorities, there is no obvious forum for resolution. But the two sides of such a debate can do more than stand opposed to one another, scream insults, and initiate legal suits. In the abortion debate, in fact, the disputants share considerable ground, and a good deal of constructive talk and argument can take place on that shared ground. Once again, the essential thing is to provide reasons and support for one's ethical position. This is not to say that our arguments should be dispassionate. Indeed, it is difficult to even think about an important moral issue without finding one's emotions already engaged. But strong conclusions—the sorts of slogans that find their way onto protest posters and bumper stickers—do not alone count as a moral position. And relativism in the lazy sense—"Oh, well, we disagree, so let's just avoid the issue"—is not a way of coming to grips with ethics. Mutual respect does not mean avoidance or cowardice. It means listening, carefully, to the opinions of those with whom one disagrees. It means cultivating and building one's own position and arguments to be evermore persuasive. And here we see the point of relativism, not limp acquiescence but genuine dialogue. Respect for one's opponent is not the same as accepting the opponent's view, nor does such respect in any way entail either giving up or weakening one's own view. Respect is not the same as agreement, though the naive relativist and the vehement critic of relativism too easily confuse them.

What about the case in which the principle of mutual tolerance itself is in question, that is, the issue of ethical relativism is itself the subject of an ethical dispute? Such a dispute puts the ethical relativist in an impossible dilemma, for a relativist cannot consistently and coherently defend mutual tolerance against someone who insists that morals are not relative, that despite the diversity of moral opinions in the world there is nevertheless a correct moral view (one's own, of course). But it does not follow, as many moralists have quickly concluded, that ethical relativism itself is an incoherent position. While it is not a coherent position applied to itself, this is a common form of paradox in the world of logic. And when the relativist and the absolutist sit down to argue for and against relativism, they engage in the dialogue and display of mutual respect that the principle of tolerance demands.

At its best, ethical relativism is itself a moral view in which the principle of tolerance is the most important moral principle, at least where other cultures or communities are concerned. On the other hand, ethical relativism can be used as an excuse for not taking any moral position seriously, including one's own. Ethical relativism can be a strategy for defusing ethical views, according to philosopher John Ladd. By answering a moral claim with the reply, "That's just your opinion," one robs it of its moral force and shifts attention from the moral claim itself to the person making the claim. In other words, it is a technique for dodging moral issues. Relativism, in its indirect way, may be just as dogmatic and intolerant as moral absolutism even while attacking dogmatism and intolerance.

Is morality ultimately justifiable? Or perhaps we should now ask, is *our* morality ultimately justifiable, where the scope of the *our* is itself in question? Ethicists often suggest that if relativism were true, then ethics would be impossible. At most, we could (like anthropologists) describe our morals, and we could continue to prescribe them, at least to one another. But we could not justify them. Our ethics would be without a foundation, and our prescriptions would be without an ultimate anchor. This fear, however, is unjustified. To think that the whole of morality turns on the question of justification and the threat of relativism is to turn ethics upside down. The process of justification may proceed from the top down, from the most abstract principles and purposes to the most particular moral judgments. But it does not follow, as many ethicists seem to believe, that the warrant of the particular judgments depends on the certainty and universality of more abstract principles. Whatever the strategy of moral justification, our moral lives proceed from the bottom up, from the ethos in which we were raised and in which most of us continue to live the whole of our lives. Indeed, it may be that we will never agree on even the formulation of the most abstract principles and purposes of morality, much less on their mode of justification. Nevertheless, within our culture, and apart from certain exceptional clashes of morals, we do agree and will continue to agree on most of our day-to-day moral decisions and judgments. And as our society becomes more and more multicultural and more and more connected to other cultures around the world, we will more and more adopt the view "live and let live" as we look for ways to get along and live well together.

Ethics does not depend on the success of philosophers's finding an adequate justification for morality as a whole. The emphasis on justification gets confused with the importance of cultivating a coherent, well-thought-out view. The importance of appreciating differences and listening to the views of others is replaced by the unnecessary and dangerous demand that we either prove them wrong or incorporate their views into our own thinking. It is the nature of justification that it always reaches further, for broader and better reasons. But ethics is not just the quest for justification, and it is not essential or perhaps even possible to step outside of one's culture and find the one or three or ten principles that are or should be fundamental to every culture and every ethical viewpoint. Indeed, we might well ask, at this point, if our concern for morality as such has become too abstract, too far removed from our day-to-day concerns and values. In our discussions of moral issues and the nature and justification of morality, something is left out. It is, to use a banal phrase, our everyday notion of a *good person* and our daily concern for living well.

THREE

Living Well: The Virtues and the Good Life

Few people believe that morality is the highest goal or the sole purpose of life. Morality, rather, provides the constraints within which we enjoy ourselves, express ourselves, make friends and acquaintances, go looking for love, strive for success and try to live our lives to the fullest. But ethics, ultimately, is about how to live and how to live well. It is not just concerned with the constraints imposed on us by morality. The questions that have been guiding us through part 2 concern the nature and justification of morality. But these questions treat morality as a distinctive phenomenon, separated from questions of good fortune, success, and happiness. Perhaps we should ask instead, How does morality fit into the good life? Much of our discussion of morality thus far has tended to treat what we *want to do* and what we *ought to do* as antagonistic rather than complementary or ultimately identical inclinations. Little has been said about what one should want and care about, about what sort of person one should strive to become. Properly understood, morality might not consist of a set of principles or rules of reason or require so much deliberation and calculation. It might be, instead, an intrinsic part of the good life, or the life well lived. Such is the assumption of a very different kind of moral theory, *virtue ethics*. On this view, living well, becoming successful, and being happy incorporate morality not as constraint but rather as a set of virtues.

Virtue ethics has been treated as a complement to traditional moral theory, and it has been defended as a radical alternative to traditional theory. The more moderate version insists only that traditional moral theory leaves something essential out of the account of our moral life and that virtue ethics supplies this. The more radical version insists that traditional moral theory is all wrong, that questions of virtue and character undermine deontological and utilitarian theories and show their accounts of moral life to be bankrupt and their vocabulary of goodness and rightness to be misleading if not fraudulent. Throughout most of part 3, we will emphasize the moderate version of virtue ethics, as a supplement to the considerations of morality we examined in part 2. But we will also discuss ways in which virtue ethics can serve not just as a supplement but as an alternative to traditional moral theory. In that regard we will look again at one of the most radical advocates of virtue ethics, the German philosopher Friedrich Nietzsche.

The Virtues

The virtues are cultivated responses and actions which may require no deliberation whatsoever. Indeed, where deontology seems to require at least some deliberation in order for us to act on principle and utilitarianism encourages even if it does not require the calculation of utilities, the expression of a virtue may to require little or no thought at all. One acts spontaneously. For example, the truly honest person probably never literally thinks of lying. Indeed, too much deliberation—"Should I be generous? Am I supposed to leave a twenty percent tip or can I get away with less?"—is evidence that one does not have the virtue in question. Many of the virtues become ridiculous if they are preceded by the sorts of deliberation encouraged by moral theorists. One does not display a sense of humor by coming to the realization that one *ought* to laugh. Of course, some virtues involve moral principles, and a thoughtful person might well generalize about his or her virtues or formulate various rules of thumb. But the virtues do not primarily rely on such thoughts and guidelines. Rather, the hallmark of a virtue is that it is engrained in one's character and, perhaps after years of cultivation and practice, seems perfectly natural.

The virtues tend to undercut the distinction between altruism and egoism that has so much preoccupied moralists and moral philosophers. A generous person may take delight in the well-being of others, but he or she need not do so. He or she may simply *be* generous, one might say overflowing, or take great pride in being a generous person. One might raise the objection that such prideful self-concern undermines or cancels out the generosity, but to be generous is simply to act and to be motivated by generosity; there is no further need to distinguish self-interest, altruism, and concern for others. To say that a person has a virtue is not to invite an investigation into his or her motives or the consequences of virtuous action. If a person routinely acts courageously, one is justified in calling him or her courageous. And whether an act of courage has good or disastrous consequences for oneself or for others, it is nevertheless an act of courage. Of course, such a claim is nullified if one discovers some unexpected ulterior motive, but we need not dig into the depths of the soul and demand purely virtuous or public-spirited motivation.

The two traditions of moral philosophy we have examined—utilitarianism and deontology—have some trouble bringing together morality and happiness, or the right and the good. Kant explicitly separated them, uniting them at the end of his philosophy only by an act of faith. Mill and the utilitarians defined the good in terms of happiness (or pleasure), but they then found themselves accused of leaving out the key concerns of morality. The emphasis on virtue and the good life which we are about to explore does not separate the right and the good at all. It begins by assuming that we are social animals whose happiness is dependent on our getting along with others and on our contributions to the community, and for whom self-esteem and self-respect are an essential ingredient in our well-being. Our well-being, accordingly, is tied to how others think of us and how we think of ourselves. Our self-interest, if we want to use that term, most often depends on being thought well of by others and being able to think well of ourselves. What makes us think well of ourselves is knowing that we are doing what we are supposed to do, not just in the sense of conforming to the rules or making our marginal contribution to the community, but by being an admirable sort of person, liked and respected by others. Doing right and making ourselves happy are one and the same. On this view the conflict of duty and self-interest is not the conceptual key to ethics but a personal problem that comes from an inadequate conception of self. According to Aristotle, the virtues are not merely means to happiness but an essential part of happiness.

A virtue, according to Socrates, is knowing and doing the right thing, for the good of one's soul. A virtue, according to David Hume, is a special trait of character that is pleasing both to other people and to ourselves. A virtue, according to Aristotle, is an "excellence," a character trait that is essential to happiness, getting along with other people, and living well in general. These different definitions suggest considerable disagreement among the philosophers who would claim that the virtues are central to ethics. Should a virtue be defined in the context of a particular society with its particular needs and values, as Hume suggests? Or is it strictly a matter of individual integrity, as Socrates argued in *Crito*. Aristotle says that a virtue is an excellence and often compares the various virtues to the skills and talents of a craftsperson or a physician; certainly a great many virtues require considerable skill, and virtually all of the virtues require cultivation and practice. As varied as these definitions are, we can safely call a virtue a desirable trait of character.

What kinds of trait are virtuous and what makes them desirable are at this point open questions.

Honesty is a virtue. So is courage. But charm and wit and a sense of humor also seem to be virtues, though not of the same sort as honesty and courage. Perhaps we should draw a sharp distinction between moral virtues, such as honesty, and nonmoral virtues, such as wit. One might suggest that the moral virtues exemplify a kind of duty, and thus should fall under a deontological analysis. Nonmoral virtues, on the other hand, are traits that are pleasing or popular, features or abilities that are useful or amusing but have nothing to do with duty. They seem to be morally optional but nonetheless make a considerable contribution to the general happiness. Thus nonmoral virtues would seem to be suited to utilitarian analysis; they are virtues insofar as they contribute to general happiness and well-being. All of those personal features that lend themselves to civility and getting along with other people—politeness, hospitality, tactfulness, an even-temper, congeniality—would be nonmoral, utilitarian virtues. Only those virtues that are obligatory and fall under a general moral rule would properly be called moral virtues.

The problem with this approach is that the virtues do not divide up that neatly into two categories, and we run the risk of falling back into the dispute between deontologists and utilitarians. Many virtues, such as loyalty and generosity, seem to be ambiguous in terms of the ongoing moral debate between Kantians and utilitarians. Are these moral virtues or not? Is a person who is disloyal acting immorally? To be sure, a person who refuses to stick with a friend, a colleague, or a company that is committing a serious crime might be said to be choosing morality over loyalty, but how are we to understand loyalty and disloyalty as such? Loyalty, unlike honesty, is tied to particular people or institutions. The imperative "Be loyal to everyone" is not intelligible. One can be loyal only to those with whom one is already engaged in one form or another. But then is loyalty to be understood in terms of a specific, acquired duty, like promise-keeping, as if loyalty were an implicit obligation or commitment? To be sure, loyalty may involve obligations, but to call loyalty as such an obligation seems to go against the spirit of the virtue. As a virtue loyalty seems different from obligation and more like love, affection, and friendship, a kind of attachment and not a duty. Likewise, if a person is ungenerous, does not give to charities and regularly undertips waiters and waitresses, would we say that he or she is immoral? Probably not, unless, perhaps, he or she were also a hypocrite, urging others to be generous and even make sacrifices while refusing to make them personally. Honesty, on the other hand, does seem to lend itself to moral judgment in a straightforward way. We easily agree that lying is immoral. But there are many forms of honesty, telling the truth when asked, for example, and volunteering the truth. The former seems like a duty, but the latter does not. Honesty may be optional; you are not obligated to tell your roommate that her new sweater simply looks awful. Honesty may serve an important purpose and further the happiness of others but not be an obligation. Indeed, honesty can even be a vice, not a virtue at all, such as when one uses the painful truth to humiliate and embarrass, to break up friendships, or to intentionally cause harm to others.

A virtue may not fulfill an obligation or contribute to the public good at all, except by way of its effects on observers. Much of what we call restraint and moderation or what Aristotle called temperance are virtues that have to do with one's desires. Consider, for example, the glutton. The glutton eats too much and may well embarrass himself or herself at the dinner table as well as friends and family. Gluttony is a vice, and the very opposite of moderation. But the vice is the gluttony itself, the excessive desire for food. It is not essential that the glutton acknowledge his or her gluttony or be embarrassed about the behavior. Even though gluttonous behavior may be all the more disgusting when it is utterly shameless and unrecognized as such by the glutton, the vice of gluttony does not depend on its effect on other people. The glutton becomes no less gluttonous by sneaking snacks in the privacy of his or her own kitchen. And gluttony is not a vice and moderation a virtue because the latter is healthy and the former detrimental to good health. Good health may be the reward of being virtuous, and being overweight and in ill health may be two of the costs of the vice, but gluttony would remain a vice even if the latest medical headlines suggested that overeating can be good for you. What constitutes gluttony is the rapacity of one's desire for food. What constitutes the virtue of moderation, on the other hand, is not holding back or resisting temptation so much as having less excessive desires in the first place. The virtue, in other words, has much more to do with what kind of a person one is than what one does. It has only secondarily to do with its effect on others, although no doubt one of the reasons that gluttony is a vice is because it disgusts other people. And moderation as a virtue has little if anything to do with duty or obligation, unless perhaps one has promised not to be gluttonous. Gluttony and moderation seem to have nothing to do with rational principles in the sense Kant describes, and they have wholly to do with what Kant called the inclinations. The glutton does not lack or fall short of any moral principle. He or she is simply a pig. Wanting too much makes a person repulsive. We need not subject the behavior to deontological or utilitarian analysis.

Of course, gluttony seems even more repulsive to us when it is combined with poor social skills and lack of consideration for other people and when we think of the millions of people in the world who are starving. One can always bolster the criticism of a vice by bringing in consequences and considering the effects on others, but social implications or consequences alone do not make something a vice or a virtue. Some excesses of desire do not affect other people at all, but we nevertheless think less of the person who indulges in them. Notice, though, that the language of disapproval tends to replace the language of right and wrong and the cost-benefit language of utilitarianism. We use critical terms such as *repulsive* and *disgusting,* or we express our repugnance through terms of amusement, disdain, and ridicule. So, too, we talk about the virtues not so much in terms of their goodness or right-ness but rather in terms of their being desirable or admirable traits. Tra-ditional terms such as *good* and *right,* whether applied to people or actions, strongly suggest a deontological or utilitarian evaluation. But the language of admiration and disgust gets us right to the heart of virtue ethics, and such talk seems to be much more the substance of our daily moral commentary than the employment of moral principles or utilitar-ian calculation.

The distinction between moral and nonmoral virtues is less impor-tant than it would seem to be from a deontological point of view. Yes, there are virtues that can be understood as applied instances of a moral principle, but not all of them are. Yes, there are virtues that are manda-tory and not at all optional, but not all virtues can be thought of in terms of duty or obligation. Whether or not a virtue is an instantiation of a moral principle or a matter of duty or obligation may well be of secondary importance. Many people seem to consider loyalty more im-portant than morality, for example, when they argue, "My country right or wrong," or when they severely chastise their friends for abandoning them in favor of their moral principles. People seem to forgive even straightforward immorality—for example, Robin Hood's thievery—if it is done in the name of generosity, a virtue. From the point of view of virtue ethics, morality is secondary to personality. This is not to say that you can be immoral if only you are sufficiently charming or to deny that conformity to moral rules is an essential aspect of character. But in vir-tue ethics a person does what he or she does because of the sort of person he or she is, whether or not there is an appropriate moral princi-ple to conform to.

Utilitarianism does not take the distinction between moral and non-moral issues all that seriously. It is more concerned with the maximiza-tion of happiness and the general good. Like virtue ethics, utilitarianism subsumes moral categories under a more general concern and does not take great pains to distinguish between what is morally right and what is good for other reasons. Thus honesty is generally good because it prevents harm, and lying is usually wrong because it does harm. But in a like manner, a sense of humor is generally good because it increases the amount of happiness in the world and the lack of one is bad because a person without humor is not only less likely to enjoy life but very likely to dampen the enjoyment of others as well. In virtue ethics, however, it is not harm and happiness that are primarily at stake but rather the praiseworthiness of a certain trait of character. Honesty is admirable, not because it is conducive to the greatest good for the greatest number or because it is a duty but because it is in itself commendable. A sense of humor is a good thing to have, not because it makes you or other people happy, (and it is certainly not a duty to laugh), but because it is in itself admirable.

Such explanations are incomplete, however, and as stated will certainly raise more questions than provide answers. Why should honesty and a sense of humor be commendable? Why not, instead, clever prevarication and dour seriousness? What does it mean to say that honesty and a sense of humor—or loyalty, generosity, and moderation—are in themselves admirable or commendable or desirable? Virtue ethics will not succeed at accounting for our moral life if it cannot back up its estimations of worth. Why are some traits virtues and other traits vices? At least deontology and utilitarianism give us answers to this question.

We can begin to answer this question by looking at the role virtues play in the living of a meaningful, fulfilling life. A virtue alone is no virtue. To be honest just for the sake of being honest or loyal just for the sake of being loyal is obstinacy, not virtue. It can even be perverse. Thus we need to link the virtues together and think of them not as isolated traits, good in themselves, but as contributions to an overall conception of character. In Aristotle, this leads to an ambitious but dubious thesis known as the *unity of the virtues*. The gist of the thesis is that you don't have any virtue if you don't have all the virtues. Thus an honest man will be loyal and generous as well. The assumption behind the thesis is that a virtue should not be a personality quirk but an essential part of an overall good character. The thesis, however, ignores or avoids the unfortunate fact that our virtues, like our moral principles, can and do sometimes come into conflict. A soldier or employee who is ordered to lie by a superior officer or manager is torn between the virtues of honesty and obedience. A friend who is asked to lie by a friend is torn between the virtues of honesty and loyalty. A host who watches a guest abuse the dog and drop ashes on the new leather sofa experiences discomfort in spite of his virtues of toleration and hospitality. Moreover, as Nietzsche in particular argued, the vigorous pursuit of one virtue may in fact eclipse or interfere with the cultivation of others, as when an artist pursues his or her creativity beyond social boundaries or when a politician pursues his or her leadership abilities into the twisted corridors of power. In all of these cases the virtues seem to be a disunity rather than a unity.

What is a Virtue?

Individual character and personal virtue are tied up in a whole way of life, or ethos. We invite disaster when we assume that virtue is virtue, that what is admired in one context will be admirable in another, or when we look only at particular virtues and ignore the life in which they play their part. Moral principles may be sufficiently broad in their application to invite such abstraction and generalization, and the principle of utility by its very nature is designed to apply to every situation in which there are sentient beings with their preferences and their interests, but virtues tend to be more specific. Because of the convoluted history of morals, the term *virtue* has become ambiguous. On the one hand, a virtue is a particular feature of a person's character, such as honesty, wittiness, generosity, or social charm. This is the sense in which we are using that term here, and, accordingly, we will typically refer to the plural *virtues*. On the other hand, *virtue* is used as an all-encompassing term; we speak of a person's virtue or talk of virtue in general, using the word as a synonym for *morality*. Kant, for example, uses *virtue* in exactly this way. Of course, a person who has virtues will very likely have virtue (be virtuous) and a virtuous person will no doubt have at least some virtues. Nevertheless, the two conceptions of virtue are distinct.

Virtue and the virtues need not go hand in hand. A person may have many virtues but nevertheless lead such a wild and unconventional life (even with no immoral behavior) that we could not call that person virtuous. On the other hand, a person, perhaps out of fear of punishment and general inhibition, may well live a life that is wholly virtuous in the moral sense, and yet be an utter bore. His or her moral character may be unblemished, but we would not necessarily regard the person as virtuous. For example, the nineteenth-century British novelist Jane Austen often creates characters who are perfectly and self-consciously proper, but they have no sense of humor or vitality whatever, and the main aim of her heroine is to avoid an impending marriage to a proper but dull man. Morality or the moral virtues alone, in other words, do not necessarily produce good character, and in the absence of other, clearly non-moral virtues, they may even be a vice. The most admirable people may lead morally ambiguous lives, and some indisputably moral people may nonetheless be impossible to admire.

If one is not willing to put the virtues ahead of morality, one might decide that the virtues are subject to moral constraints. A deontologist might adopt virtue ethics as a complement to duty and autonomy, admitting that the virtues are what make social life livable and that they define what we consider to be good character, but only within moral parameters that are not themselves matters of virtue. In this view, virtue might be thought of as social skills and entertaining or useful social habits, which the deontologist might well admit are necessary to being a good person. Indeed, the deontologist might also concede that one cannot make a sharp distinction between moral and nonmoral virtues. Honesty as a virtue is not merely a manifestation of the duty to tell the truth and, as a virtue, it need not be considered moral. But, whatever the virtue, it must be morally acceptable. An exceptional ability to charm and swindle the shirt off of unsuspecting strangers could not be a virtue, no matter what the context, just as the ability to kill children with a slingshot could not count as a virtue, even if it were admired or enjoyed by some particularly demented subgroup of society. Thus, the deontologist might well accept a moderate view of virtue ethics, adding only the stipulation that virtue must conform to or at least not conflict with morality. So, too, the utilitarian might insist that a virtue, whatever else its features, must enhance or at least not interfere with general well-being. Both the deontologist and the utilitarian could agree that the virtues are important and should be understood independently of duty and utility respectively, but they would insist that morality and the public good are, nevertheless, primary.

The compromise position on the role of virtue in ethics, however, does have a drawback. Requiring that a virtue should not be immoral or harmful renders the concept of virtue secondary and inessential to ethics. This view declares that virtues are good things to have because they are pleasant or enjoyable or even exciting, but they are as such only embellishments and details in our moral life, subject to the constraints of morality and the interests of utility. A more radical position on the virtues is that they are desirable for their own sake and do not depend on morality and utility for their legitimacy. They may even conflict with morality and utility. The point is not that good citizens should be something more than dull rule-followers. The point is that admirable people are something more than moral or useful.

Nevertheless, what counts as a virtue certainly depends on the nature of the society in which it is embedded as well as on the overall character in whom it plays its role. Hume may be correct in saying that a virtue is a feature that is particularly pleasing and desirable to others, but it certainly depends on the nature of the context and the culture of the society in question. What was pleasing to Hume and his gentlemen friends in Edinburgh were, understandably, the virtues of a gentleman. What was pleasing to Agamemnon on the battlefield in front of the walls of Troy was a set of virtues that were certainly not gentlemanly. The fact that a virtue must be considered admirable within the context of one's particular society means that the virtues may well vary from context to context, whether they serve some specific practical function, such as having good business sense in the corporate world or knowing how to handle snakes on a snake farm, or whether they appeal to the particular ideals of a culture. Being devout and faithful will be among the greatest virtues in a religious society. Being creative and even eccentric will be virtues in a society of artists or academics in which originality and individuality are celebrated. Being honorable and acting honorably will be among the highest virtues in a society such as Japan, in which proper behavior is often precisely described and public shame may be worse than death.

Virtues can also become outmoded. Being able to fight well with a sword and being the fastest gun in the West are no longer virtues in late twentieth-century America. At most, they might be salable skills in Hollywood. Having a pacifist's distaste for violence would not have been a virtue during the Trojan War and having a superb sense of humor would not have been a virtue in a medieval Carmelite monastery. The aging of virtues is almost always resisted and deplored as a loss of values, but as societies change (not necessarily for the better), the virtues will tend to change too. What once was a virtue may well become a vice, and what was a vice for one generation may well become a virtue for the next.

Philosophers have often argued that morality is defined in part by its universality, but few ethicists have been tempted to say that about the virtues. Indeed, the most striking thing about the virtues is how they vary from culture to culture and throughout history. Many Americans value a sense of humor, comedy, and a good laugh, but in some other societies humor is less important and raucous laughter is considered both foolish and obnoxious. Americans, on the other hand, generally tend to avoid discussions and rituals having to do with death, but in many cultures the dead and ideas about death play a large part in daily life. The ancient Egyptians for example, had elaborate daily rituals concerning death. In America, people in mourning are often ignored, or merely tolerated, and if the mourning process goes on very long, the person in mourning may be criticized or urged to seek psychiatric help. In other societies mourning may be expected to last a lifetime and the American attitude might be considered irreverent or pathological. Thus the capacity to mourn is a virtue in some societies and not a virtue, or less of a virtue, in others.

To understand why this can be so, we need to look at the overall social context. Death is an ineradicable aspect of the human condition. But what most Americans mean by death, whatever their religious convictions and beliefs about the afterlife, is quite different from the idea of death in those societies that emphasize mourning rituals. For most Americans death is considered an individual or family tragedy. In many other societies death is also a social misfortune and part of the predictable ebb and flow of communal life. One can lament the lack of community and larger family-feeling among many Americans and criticize the lack of comprehension and compassion concerning death that an absence of established mourning rituals may indicate. But the absence of certain virtues regarding death (for which we do not even have names) is part of an overall conception of life, and one cannot criticize the virtues (or the lack of them) without taking that conception into consideration.

The virtues are part of a way of life. To suppose that the virtues are the same the world over is to presume that lives are lived in the same way everywhere and that all people consider the same things important and valuable. Even where universal aspects of the human condition are examined, societies vary enormously. Everyone has to eat, but different societies eat very different foods in very different ways and may attach a very different significance to eating. A favorite delicacy in one culture may be taboo in another. What counts as gluttony or bad manners in one society may be considered polite and appreciative behavior in another. Almost all societies reproduce themselves, but even the act of reproduction has very different and usually very complex meanings and constraints in different cultures and, accordingly, is associated with very different virtues and vices. In the realm of religious and social conventions, we can expect considerable and sometimes violent differences in the understanding of the virtues. To take but one example, which we will explore in some depth shortly, the virtues of a highly stratified society, in which an aristocracy presumes a certain superiority and has the necessities of life taken care of by others, is going to emphasize very different virtues than a society that is egalitarian.

But surely there are some common virtues, if only those that are essential to the survival and stability of society as such. Even here we find significant differences. Cooperativeness would seem to be a universal virtue, but the free market system highlights the opposite virtue, competitiveness. Of course, a free market presupposes cooperation, but the point is that even the basic virtues of congeniality and getting along together can be understood in very different ways. So, too, with such seemingly universal virtues as courage and generosity. Courage in Homer's Greece could be measured by one's stalwart behavior in hand-to-hand combat, and even Aristotle insists that the only true measure of courage is on the battlefield. In twentieth-century America we most often mention courage in the context of the "courage of one's convictions." That is hardly the same virtue as the courage of Achilles facing a hundred Trojans in battle. Generosity in modern societies with a wealthy class may refer to an overflowing of wealth which spills out to feed the hungry and help the needy or subsidize art exhibits and operas. In medieval society, generosity entailed personal sacrifice, as when Thomas Becket gave away everything he owned to the poor. And among some native American tribes generosity is expressed in the ritual of *pot-latch,* a competition to see who can give away more than anyone else, as a matter of status and honor. Does one need to make a considerable sacrifice to be generous? Do these three examples reflect the same notion of generosity? The same virtue? Again, to adequately understand the virtue one needs to take the overall social context into account. But even considering the similarities and differences among societies, the idea that there is one overriding measure of virtue seems implausible at best.

To get a concrete idea of at least one well-developed list of virtues, let us consider a well-known list that comes from Aristotle. His list reflects the virtues of Athenian society at a particular moment in its history. It is important to keep in mind that Aristotle's Greece was no longer the Greece of Homer's *Iliad;* the Athenians were no longer a crude tribe in conflict with other crude tribes. Athens was a *polis,* a free and sophisticated city-state, at least when compared with any other society in ancient history, with a representative government and a rich heritage of art, philosophy, and statesmanship. Aristotle's list of the virtues sums up the Athenian notion of honor, which includes being held in high public esteem as well as always acting in such a way that one's good name will never be challenged. This is a very different conception of virtue from the warrior virtues of the *Iliad,* in which physical domination rather than successful civility was the measure of one's public status. (Achilles and Agamemnon, two heroes of the Trojan War, would have been considered barbarians in Aristotle's Athens.)

Here is Aristotle's list of virtues:

Courage	Friendliness
Temperance	Truthfulness
Liberality	Wittiness
Magnificence	Shame
Pride	Justice
Good temper	

One of the first things we may notice about this list of virtues is that it includes some virtues which we would not consider as such, pride, for instance. We often think of pride as a kind of egotism, or at best as a kind of defensiveness. The closest sense we have of Aristotle's *pride* is expressed in the question, "Have you no pride?" But Aristotle means more than the refusal to humiliate oneself. To be proud is to have self-esteem, but it is not just to feel good about oneself, as we might say; it is to see oneself as superior, because one *is* superior. Without being smug or condescending, one should fully acknowledge and enjoy one's stature in the community. Aristotle's fellow Athenians would not consider humility a virtue at all, but rather a vice, a sign of weakness or insipidness.

The list also omits certain cardinal Christian virtues, faith and hope, for example. Charity is, in a way, included in liberality, but that is quite different from the Christian virtue. Liberality is an overflowing, self-sufficiency coupled with abundance. The Christian notion of charity by contrast involves self-sacrifice and a keen awareness of our connection to the poor. Magnificence, or giving great public parties, is not the same as amiability and hospitality in our much more private and personal sense. A good temper may be a desirable virtue in a neighbor who is armed with a sword, but it is not the same as the warmth and good neighborliness that many Americans praise today. Indeed, it is probably safe to say that a modern American visitor to ancient Athens would very likely be appalled by the society we have so idealized and idolized for so many centuries. We would not recognize many of the Aristotlean virtues as virtues at all.

The names of the virtues in the list are often misleading not only because of the usual difficulties of translation but also because of the many differences between the ancient Greek culture and our own. Temperance, for example, does not refer to abstinence but only to moderation. Indeed, Aristotle and his friends would have looked upon someone who refused on principle to indulge in wine, sex, and song as an insufferable bore. And friendliness for Aristotle is not at all our give-a-healthy-handshake-and-a-big-smile variety. Friendliness refers more to being a friend than to any particular feeling or expression of friendship. It certainly does not mean being friendly to everybody.

Aristotle sometimes says that the good person has all the virtues, and that one cannot have any of them without having all of them. His claim for the unity of the virtues may be overstated, but we can accept that virtues are often interrelated. He also says that virtue develops from a certain good upbringing and self-control. The virtues in general, he argues, are "means between the extremes," and one must be raised to have the right perceptions as well as to perform the right actions. To know the mean between the extremes is to have and act on the correct amount of emotion or desire, for example. For example, temperance involves a moderate but not negligible amount of desire, while gluttony involves much too much desire and abstemiousness too little. Courage is the mean between cowardice and foolhardiness, where cowardice is having too much fear and foolhardiness too little. Notice that, by this account, courage is not the same as fearlessness. Indeed, fearlessness, of the sort depicted in many American movies, would be considered by Aristotle to be either foolhardiness or wishful fiction. A virtue, he says, is "a state of character." It is not just an isolated trait or feature of our behavior, however benign. It is not merely doing the right thing at the right time, and it is not merely a passing passion. For Aristotle, a virtue is something drilled into us along with all of the other virtues since childhood and is now a matter of habit. Indeed, the idea that a person should struggle to be virtuous would strike Aristotle as nonsense; to have a virtue means that one acts virtuously naturally, without struggle or moral turmoil. The test of virtue, according to Aristotle, is that one enjoys its exercise. It is no virtue when a person forces himself to do something. Furthermore, the virtue and its exercise fits in with all of the other virtues as well. Aristotle has in mind an ideal borrowed from Plato, the harmony of the soul. Harmony requires coherence, and the most obvious way to have a coherent, harmonious soul is to have all the virtues in a single package, cultivated in us as second nature since childhood.

The idea that virtue is primarily a matter of good upbringing and becomes second nature as well as the ideal of harmony marks an important shift away from traditional moral theories. Of course, no deontologist or utilitarian would deny the importance of moral education, and the utilitarian, at least, would absorb the ideal of harmony under the heading of happiness. But Aristotle's virtues are formulated around a certain kind of life. Ethics is a question of one's whole character, not just a question of this virtue or that. And because they are part of a particular way of life, these virtues and the happiness they yield are not available to anyone. Indeed, Aristotle thought that barbarians could not have any of the virtues because they did not grow up and live in so sophisticated a society as the Greek polis. He might well think that of us too.

The virtues listed by Aristotle are the virtues of well-educated, aristocratic, male Athenian citizens. Women in Athens did not have the freedom, the education or the status to strive for such ideals. Slaves, of course, could be nothing more than "good slaves," according to Aristotle. Children were not to be called virtuous or happy; they were pre-adults, whose virtuousness and happiness could be judged only later. And because Aristotle was an aristocrat who disdained physical labor and depended for the necessities of life on those who had the demeaning tasks of providing them, Aristotle also ignores the virtues of hard work and perseverance. He also expresses nothing but scorn for what we would call the commercial virtues, or the virtues of business, and he would have considered much of the protestant work ethic and what Americans consider success to be depraved. So, as appealing as it may be to some, the prospect of simply adopting Aristotle's conception and list of the virtues is neither plausible nor politically possible. What we can do, however, is return to the heart of Aristotle's ethics, appreciate how his conception of the virtues developed out of the practices and traditions of his society, and develop a conception of the virtues that is appropriate to modern democratic society.

Virtues and Vices: Practices and Tradition

Virtues tend to be more or less specific to certain practices and traditions. Aristotle's list of virtues is quite explicitly limited to that small class of male Athenian aristocrats whose role in the polis was leadership and statesmanship. There were other virtues for ordinary soldiers and for craftsmen, for wives, for slaves, and for farmers. The virtues, obviously, were not only good in themselves and desirable for their own sake. They were functional. They served a purpose in the society in which they played a part. This is not to say that they necessarily served the general utility, for societies may have purposes quite apart from matters of utility or the public good, and those purposes or their realization may or may not make people happier or give them pleasure or satisfy them in an obvious way. But the concepts of function and purpose provide a large part of our answer to the question, What makes a virtue a virtue? We do not need to appeal to either general rules of morality or to considerations of utility and general welfare. We should, rather, look at the ideals of a particular society, or what inspires and ultimately motivates its most admirable members.

In his book, *After Virtue,* Alasdair MacIntyre provides an extensive analysis of the concept of virtue and the variety of virtues that we find in history from Homer to the Victorians. A virtue, he tells us, is not merely an admirable trait in a particular society. It is, rather, one of the cardinal features of a *practice,* a specific goal-oriented activity that carries with it a certain tradition, an established way of doing and thinking about things. A game of chess might be an example of such a practice.

Chess is a practice that has evolved over centuries. When you sit down at a chess board with a friend, you do not invent the rules or the goals of the game; they are already there for you, along with the pieces and their designated moves and a long tradition of tried and sometimes true strategies for winning. Accordingly, what we might call the virtues of a chess player are determined by the strategic nature of the practice. We can imagine a tradition in which that practice and its virtues would be very different, for example, if the object of the game were to shoot the tops off the pieces with shotguns, but within the practice and tradition that we call chess the goals and the virtues of the game are quite clear and thoroughly settled.

What we have called an ethos is a combination of various practices and traditions, cultivated over time and defining certain virtues as especially desirable features. The very notion of a virtue presupposes a set of ideals, a sense of what people in a particular society are supposed to strive for and admire. The virtues may be very rare in practice, as some Christian saints have exemplified, or they may be fairly common, as Aristotle considered the Athenian virtues to be among the aristocracy. But virtues represent the ideals of a particular ethos, its conception of its own ultimate purpose, or telos. Aristotle saw his society primarily in political terms, from the point of view of an enlightened but embattled aristocracy trying to survive, whose members were trying to get on well with one another. A medieval monastery recognized its telos in God, and its virtues were therefore piety and faith. Most Americans see society's function as maximizing happiness and prosperity. Our virtues, accordingly, tend to be psychological and economic—hard work, efficiency, a keen sense of play, and good use of leisure time.

Virtues, in general, develop because they are useful to the society of which they are an essential part, but a virtue may long outlive its usefulness and yet continue to play an essential role in the life of a community. What was once fully functional may now serve as an important ritual that helps hold the society together and gives its members shared meaning and focus. What is most useful and necessary to the life of a community, on the other hand, may not be considered as virtue. Aristotle's Athens had an agrarian economy, for example, but Aristotle never mentioned the virtues of farming. Until very recently, many Americans assumed that their natural environment was an unlimited resource which could be used as needed and abused without worry; what we now recognize as essential ecological virtues were either unrecognized or ridiculed as an odd eccentricity of certain "nature lovers." Now, confronted with environmental ruin, we are developing or adopting new practices and new attitudes and new virtues to go with them. Necessity is not only the mother of invention; it may also be the mother of virtue.

In our pluralistic society it would be highly implausible to suggest that there is a single set of virtues and vices for everyone. At the same time it is absurd to suggest, as many self-help psychology books do, that each of us has his or her own unique virtues. (Nietzsche offers this view in his long prose-poem *Thus Spoke Zarathustra*.) Some very general virtues have to do with just basically getting along with others, especially the virtue of tolerance, but even this virtue is not shared by all groups or is extensively qualified, as in the moral debate on abortion. But for the most part, we can understand the virtues and the vices if we focus on particular communities and practices. In any community or practice, there will be more or less well-defined contexts or traditions in which certain clusters of virtues and vices become evident. These will, to a considerable extent, be functional and help the group to hold together and survive, sometimes by keeping out those who would subvert the purposes of the practice and split the community.

Consider, for example, the college or university community and its scholarly virtues. The virtues listed below are essential to studying and research, but they are also highly functional in reinforcing certain group standards and keeping out or eliminating those who do not follow them:

Being attentive and thorough, paying attention to details

Being trained or competent in a chosen subject

Being thoughtful and organized

Having something to say that is new and interesting

Being clear and providing adequate argument and evidence

Being serious (no fooling around)

Being honest, quoting accurately, and giving credit where it is due

We can readily understand why these traits should be virtues in the scholarly community, which includes students, of course. We can also see how these virtues would not be appropriate in another context, for example, in amateur sports or in an organization whose primary purpose is to provide fun and games for its members. Of course, the contemporary college or university embraces all three of these contexts—scholarship, sports, and social clubs, and there can be considerable friction between them, as every college or university president knows all too well. But in terms of scholarship and its application to teaching, the role and function of the virtues is amply clear. The overriding telos is learning. Learning does not, presumably, preclude having fun, but entertainment and enjoyment are to be encouraged or tolerated only to the extent that they aid learning. Nor does this telos eliminate competition but, again, competition for grades and, at the professorial level, for grants and recognition is encouraged or tolerated only to the extent that this competition furthers learning. What learning requires is, first and foremost, attentiveness. Accordingly, the first virtue of scholarship is paying attention. But a blank stare doesn't count as a virtue; it is necessary to pay attention to details, to be thorough. A student should read other books on the subject. A scholar should read as many books on the subject as possible. A researcher sifts through all the evidence, not just the evidence initially favorable to his or her conclusion. He or she does not neglect or ignore competing hypotheses or interpretations.

In a scholarly community training in a subject is also essential. Naivete in a student may be acceptable in an introductory class, but it wears thin soon and can become humiliating for a student. Competence is important in the area of research too. No field can proceed or stay intact if there are no standards for measuring competence, and no way of distinguishing good sense and solid work from flim-flam and incompetence. Competence is an essential virtue but it is also a minimal one. To call a student or colleague merely competent in a letter of recommendation is to kill with faint praise. Thus, if competence is a virtue, then genius and mastery are ideals, of which competence is merely a pathetic shadow.

Being thoughtful and organized is also a pedestrian virtue but nevertheless essential. In writing one must have a thesis and a plan; one can't just throw together a lot of facts and figures that don't add up to anything.

Having something to say that is new, surprising, or thought-provoking may not be a virtue it itself—rather, it seems like an accomplishment—but originality and creativity, or at least being in a position to recognize originality and creativity when one sees it, surely counts as a scholarly virtue. Originality and creativity are often fused with profundity and deep thinking, but what is often presented as deep is only unintelligible; as Nietzsche said of the romantics of his time, "They muddy the waters in order that they look deep." Being clear and presenting your research so that it is easily understood is, in academia, an often neglected virtue that is akin to congeniality. On the other hand, merely stating the obvious or the superficial, however clear and easy to understand, is no virtue either.

Being serious is a virtue that is greatly overrated, but it is surely essential to have the conviction that what one is doing is important. Humor has its place in academia, perhaps, but it should never undermine the worth of the study itself.

Being honest is a sometimes-neglected virtue among students and researchers, who find that the competition for grades and grants is getting too keen. But giving proper credit for sources and stating the facts as you find them, not making them up as you need them, is basic to learning. Plagiarism, accordingly, is not just cheating, and it is not just the violation of a moral rule. As Kant argues, widespread cheating may undermine the very institution it was meant to take advantage of, and, as a rule utilitarian might argue, cheating ultimately hurts everyone. In virtue ethics the person who pretends that other people's words are his or her own is a person who merely pretends to learn instead of pursuing learning, and therefore isn't the sort of person who belongs in the university community.

When we discuss virtues in general, they can become vague and we can begin to think that almost anything can be a virtue somewhere, under some conditions, but when we look at particular communities and their practices, this vagueness is dispelled and the virtues emerge with remarkable clarity and strictness. There is always room for disagreement, of course, and some will always challenge even the most prestigious and central virtues of any practice and suggest alternatives. But these alternatives typically represent other virtues of the practice, and the argument is often one of emphasis. For example, maverick professors may employ unusual teaching techniques to stimulate original thinking in their students, sacrificing some of the traditional scholarly propriety and seriousness. But the ultimate telos, learning, remains the same. One can gain a similar understanding of the virtues by looking at any specific community or practice, whether it is football, foreign diplomacy, or fraternity pledging and initiation, and outlining its essential virtues and vices. If the larger theory of virtue ethics seems open and formless, the precision of virtue ethics on context is striking.

Many proponents of virtue ethics, however, still hold out the hope of finding a single set of virtues and vices that define good and bad people as such, apart from any particular community or tradition. At one extreme they maintain that a certain constellation of vices would exclude someone from virtually any community or society. Certainly someone who is selfish, inconsiderate, hostile to everyone, disrespectful of all rules, indifferent to considerations of fairness, honesty, truth, and taste will tend to be unwelcome and potentially destructive in any group or practice. But it is important to resist the temptation to reach for an all-embracing theory, and not just for the sake of respecting multicultural differences. Almost every practice allows for certain exceptions, not just the maverick who shifts the shape of the practice but also the eccentric who creates a certain internal disruption and disharmony. In academia and the art world, perhaps, the celebration of eccentricity is more commonplace. But other communities and practices have eccentrics too, and though such eccentrics may be intolerable in large numbers, they serve an important function. One example is the "wise guy," the person who, while participating in a practice (and perhaps participating in it much more seriously than he or she seems to), makes fun of it and disrupts it. Several wise guys would destroy any practice (even the practice of being a wise guy), but the presence of one such person allows everyone else to relax a bit and get a perspective on this practice that might otherwise be lost. Indeed, what would an American high school class be like without a wise guy? Another example is the eccentric genius who risks ostracized and being made fun of for wanting to take a practice beyond its current limits. Again, no practice can consist wholly of eccentrics, even geniuses, but a few eccentrics or geniuses keep a practice alive and invigorating. To insist that the virtues consist of those characteristics that everyone should have in a practice or in a society with a plurality of practices is to miss the importance of the exceptions. But, at the same time, to insist that everyone be an exception and to celebrate only the eccentric virtues is an absurdity. The virtues are bound to our practices, and it is only due to the cooperation and acceptance within a practice that there can be virtues at all. On the other hand, the virtues are as varied as our practices, and it is the variety of characters and practices that we consider, as a society and as individuals, to be our greatest virtue.

Happiness and the Good Life: Satisfaction and Self-esteem

The promise of virtue ethics is that it can bring together the demands of morality and the pursuit of happiness. We have, thus far, discussed the nature of the virtues with respect to morals, but we have not yet explored the notion of happiness. Living the good life, on the one hand, surely means doing good, acting in the right way, having the virtues. On the other hand, the good life also means living well, getting some pleasure out of life, and enjoying oneself, that is, being happy. But what is happiness? And how does happiness relate to the virtues?

According to Aristotle, the two are related virtually by definition. Happiness is simply the name of the good life, and it subsumes the virtues as an essential part of its character. "Happiness is the life of activity in accordance with virtue," he tells us. But the word *happiness* can be misleading. It seems to be something quite concrete and specific, but in fact it covers a great deal of territory. We often talk as if happiness were a particular feeling, but happiness is not merely the momentary feeling of being happy; it is the overall measure of a good life. Aristotle tells us that happiness (*eudaimonia*) is nothing more than the name of the ultimate good or telos in life, that toward which all our activities and hopes are aimed.

What particular goals, activities, and achievements constitute happiness? *Eudaimonia* is often translated as "doing well" or "flourishing," suggesting that success and happiness are one and the same. Of course, here success means something more than simply doing well in one's career or earning a good deal of money. The good life, Aristotle tells us, is defined in part by one's status and respect in the community, the esteem in which one is held by his or her fellows. The Greek term for virtue (*arete*) is often translated as "excellence." To be good at what one does and to be a good person are thus intricately tied together, and

Aristotle would have little patience or understanding for people who wholly divorce their work from their personal life. Furthermore, living well means living together. Political participation in one's community thus, is more than merely an obligation or an unpleasant necessity; it is part of living well.

Notice how Aristotle ties all of the concepts related to the good life so closely together that it becomes impossible to make our modern distinctions between self-interest and altruism, the personal and the social, or success and happiness. Perhaps because we tend to separate these concepts, we create so many moral crises and conflicts of interest. We distinguish and separate morality and happiness and then overemphasize the threat of or the need for self-sacrifice. We separate success and virtue and then complain about the number of unscrupulous professionals, and we wonder how a person can keep his or her integrity and be successful. Aristotle, by contrast, avoids these polarities. The good life is being virtuous and happy and not just being moral. In Aristotle, virtue is already part and parcel of happiness, while the Kantian conception of morality separates the two. Of course, being virtuous does not guarantee happiness—one can always be struck by tragedy despite one's virtues—but there can be no happiness without virtue.

Many hedonists would say that the good life is the life of pleasure. Many moralists, in response, would be horrified. But Aristotle would not wholly disagree with the hedonists. One could not be happy without pleasure in life. The test of having a virtue, according to Aristotle, is that one enjoys its exercise. To live the virtuous life is already to enjoy life, to be pleased with oneself and who one is. One does not have to force oneself to be virtuous, and one does not have to overcome temptation. While the glutton certainly enjoys food, the virtuous person also enjoys food, though in moderate amounts. Being virtuous does not mean giving up what one wants. To be virtuous is to want to be virtuous, and so the choice between doing what one wants to do and doing what one ought to do does not even arise. And because virtue is also excellence, the good life for Aristotle is an active life in which we are virtuous by doing our best in those activities that allow us to contribute to society and ensure our own health and well-being. We are not forced to choose between virtue and success. In Aristotle's ethics, there is no room for the careerist whose ambitions eclipse his sense of virtue, just as there would be no room for a so-called moral person, who by leading a timid and minimal life, did nothing wrong only because he or she did virtually nothing.

Because of Aristotle's own role as philosopher and his close association with the great statesmen of Athens, the virtues he listed were particularly appropriate for such men, and the accomplishments he was thinking of were largely in the public realm of politics and statesmanship. He more or less took for granted the accomplishments of everyone else in society and virtually ignored the idea that they too could be happy. Of course, he acknowledged that servants, soldiers, farmers, and shoemakers could have virtues, but these were only the virtues related to their servile status, and these people could be happy, at best, in some inferior sense. They could do their work and play their roles well and be content with their lives. But Aristotle equated the virtues and happiness of the aristocratic class with the virtues and good life of the excellent human being. Today we would not accept the notion that the best life is necessarily the life of the wealthy and privileged rulers. Thus, if denying the possibility of happiness in the fullest sense to servants, soldiers, farmers, and shoemakers we are to make use of Aristotle's notion of happiness, we must expand our vision and insist that happiness and the good life do not depend on having the good fortune to be born into the upper crust of society.

Aristotle has, understandably, often been called an elitist, and indeed he wrote his ethics not for everyone but for the elite. (The word *aristocracy* means "rule by the best.") But Aristotle's insistence on the connection between happiness, virtue, and excellence can apply to people at all levels of society. What is important is that one does whatever one does as well as possible and thus makes his or her contribution to the community. Nevertheless, to think that everyone can be happy and anyone can be virtuous may show unwarranted optimism. Both happiness and virtue have preconditions, and perhaps a good or at least decent upbringing is one of them. Some individuals suffering under the most severe handicaps—chronic disease, extreme poverty, social unrest— have still managed to make themselves both virtuous and happy, but the good life, among both the advantaged and the disadvantaged, is probably relatively rare accomplishment.

The exemplary hero, for Aristotle, was Socrates. (Socrates was no aristocrat, though most of his students were.) Socrates presents us with an example that is both exhilarating and disturbing. He lived a long, healthy, vigorous life. He enjoyed many pleasures. Indeed, he seemed to enjoy just about everything. Most of all, he loved the personal interaction of arguing about philosophy with the brightest young men of Athens. It was like a contest to him, and he was no doubt the best. In the end, he chose to die, not because he did not love life but, on the contrary, because he loved it so much. He died, he tells us, for the sake of his soul, which he believed to be eternal. He may have had years of pleasure ahead of him had he chosen to escape from prison, but he believed his life would no longer have been meaningful. He would have betrayed the thing that gave it significance. Socrates's extreme example underscores what is true for all of us, that living well is not just living a pleasurable life. It is living a full and meaningful life. Socrates did not distinguish between his life as a whole, his happiness, and his virtues. To say that he died for the sake of his soul meant that his death was an essential and necessary part of his life. Accepting death to make an important philosophical point was as natural for him as winning an argument or falling asleep at the end of a long day.

Not everyone, of course, is a Socrates. It is by no means easy to take him as a model, and even if one does, it is difficult to know how one should live in order to emulate him. He was, one might say, one of a kind. But if we cannot be like Socrates, we can still find a way to be exemplary. Indeed, one of the more appealing features of an ethics of virtue is that each of us is one of a kind, in that the exact composition of virtues and excellences that makes one person exemplary is not the same as that of another exemplary person. For some people, happiness and the good life are conceived in terms of security and raising a family, while others see life as the opportunity to exercise their creativity through art. The question is whether one lives a fulfilling virtuous life in pursuit of the goals one has chosen. Some people seek power and prestige. There may be nothing wrong with this, but one needs to have a clear conception of why such goals are so important and how they can be virtuously pursued. Power, in particular, is a means, and it always invites the question, What will the power accomplish? Some people seek knowledge or adventure, some just want to be liked and respected by their friends, and some seem to be satisfied just seeking entertainment, which may involve virtues such as taste and sociability.

Every life contains its own possibilities for happiness, its own virtues, depending on the practice and the community in which a person participates. The advantage of the more egalitarian analysis of virtue is that there is no need to evaluate our lives in terms of someone else's inappropriate standards or in terms so all-embracing that we need to feel left out, unhappy or unvirtuous. We all participate in various practices. Doing well or flourishing means succeeding in those practices in accordance with the virtues of the practice and enjoying our success as well. We aim at excellence and virtue not because we have to but because we want to, because that is what defines who we are and who we want to be. This is not to say that anything can be a virtue, given the appropriate context, nor is it to say that skills and talents that are merely professional and not at all personal count as virtues. Being a good parent is a virtue; being a good accountant is not. Being kind and generous are virtues; being clever and skillful at sifting through evidence is not. Bear in mind, though, that the professional and the personal frequently overlap. It is, perhaps, one of the ethical maladies of our times that we overemphasize work and isolate our careers from the more personal parts of our lives. As Aristotle maintained, happiness and the good life essentially involve love, family, and friendship as well as what we broadly call success.

One of the problems that Aristotle pondered but perhaps did not solve is what we might call the problem of priorities. Aristotle, like many philosophers following him, suggested that the goal for all of us is happiness, but he is quite clear that this goal does not in itself dictate any particular way to live and includes a great many ingredients in various proportions. Aristotle was somewhat ambivalent about what he thought was the best way to live. In some of his writings he suggests that the best life is the life of contemplation, which suggests a relatively solitary and inactive life of study, thought, and reflection. Elsewhere he argues that the best life is a full, active, social life, in which thought and reflection play some role but by no means dominate our time or our attention. Readers of Aristotle today have disputed what he meant by the life of contemplation and what he calls the intellectual virtues, although he surely does not recommend being a hermit. This tension in Aristotle's ethics between philosophical thought and public life suggests a danger that threatens all of us. It is usually easy enough to pick one ingredient of the good life that seems more important to us than any of the others—artistic achievement or success or athletic accomplishment, for example. But it is not so easy to see how we can fit in all of the other parts of the good life, such as quiet moments of contemplation or relaxation or meaningful time with friends and family. For Aristotle, the problem was how to be a full-time philosopher and at the same time be a complete human being. For many of us, the problem is how to be dedicated and successful in school or on the job and simultaneously satisfied and fulfilled in our personal lives. The question, "What is the good life and how should I live?" is very much an open question, and no single set of virtues, ambitions, or accomplishments provides the answer for everyone.

This problem of priorities—how to give proper weight to competing demands on our attention and our talents—seems to have increased in the past century or so. The German playwright and philosopher Friedrich Schelling complained about the fragmentation of life at the turn of the nineteenth century, followed by Karl Marx who fantasized about the time when "man could once again be a fisherman in the morning, a hunter in the afternoon," and no longer be restricted by the narrow specialization of modern life. We would like to think of what Aristotle called the good life as a single universal goal, common to ancient Greeks, medieval Chinese, and modern Americans, but we are aware of cultural differences, and the legitimacy of these differences, in a way that Aristotle was not. One central characteristic of our own circumstances is the specialization of our lives, the fact that most of us are expected to do one sort of thing and spend at least half our adult waking lives doing it. Specialization is a fact of life more than ever before: "I can't do everything, so what things should I do?" Ours may seem to be a life richer than almost any ever known before, but it is also a life of roads considered but not taken, doors slammed shut, and ordinary experiences unknown and untried. This makes ethics an exceptionally important enterprise, for there is a sense in which what we are choosing when we choose a career—whether medicine or business, entertainment or law—is an ethos, a way of life, with a set of goals and values that go with it.

Even if we agree that happiness is a life of activity in accordance with virtue, many questions still remain unanswered. For example, what is the role of desire and satisfaction in the good life? Happiness is often thought of as the satisfaction of all (or at least most of) our desires. Of course, it would be absurd to say that a person is flourishing if virtually all his or her desires were frustrated and all of his or her ambitions ended in failure. But there are at least three reasons to qualify the apparently plausible view that happiness is the satisfaction of our desires. First, satisfying our desires is not strictly a matter of self-interest. Many of our desires are bound up with the desires and happiness of others. One's happiness may depend on the well-being of one's family, or the success of one's business firm, or the flourishing of the community. These goals may still be the object of one's desires, but it would be misleading to suggest that happiness is just the satisfaction of one's own desires; it may be the satisfaction of other people's desires and other standards and goals as well. Indeed, this fact led Aristotle to make the odd suggestion that a person's happiness continues after he or she is dead, for the goals and standards desired in life—for example, the success and happiness of one's children—continue after one's life is over. Of course, this concept would make no sense at all if one were to think of happiness as a feeling.

The second reason for hesitating to accept the view that happiness is the satisfaction of desires is the insatiability of some of the most important desires in life. They are never satisfied. Artists and writers are rarely satisfied once and for all. They often feel that each work is a step toward a final goal they never achieve. Very religious people often insist that faith is more quest than conquest. Perfect faith, while an ideal to be striven for all one's life, is never actually attainable. Even the pursuit of pleasure may never be satisfied. The great German poet Goethe has his lecherous character Faust exclaim, "From desire I rush to satisfaction, but from satisfaction I leap to desire." Happiness, in other words, need not be the product of our efforts but may be those efforts themselves. Or, as a French wit once put it, "Love desires not satisfaction but prolongation." So it may be with life and happiness; not satisfaction but lifelong effort and continuing passion are what count.

The third reason for not thinking of happiness as the satisfaction of our desires depends on the all-important difference between the satisfaction of our desires and the satisfaction of ourselves. Self-satisfaction includes the satisfaction of a good many goals and ambitions, but this overall self-satisfaction, which incorporates our concern for the well-being of others and the ethos of our community, is what makes a whole life and gives it integrity. For example, when it came down to the hardest decision of all, Socrates decided to forfeit his life in return for something much more abstract and intangible. He claimed that he accepted an unjust death for the sake of his soul. In less religious language, we might say that he died for the sake of his integrity, his wholeness as a person, his sense of who he was. He satisfied himself in doing what he believed to be right and in exemplifying virtue.

Philosophers and psychologists are forever finding new motives behind everything that we do—pleasure, power, sex, selfishness—but much of what we do is motivated by our concern with the self, an effort to feel better about ourselves and our place among our peers. How we feel about ourselves is called *self-esteem*. How we feel about ourselves with respect to our peers is *self-respect*. Both are essential to happiness and the good life. Both are tied to the virtues. But the difference between the two is significant also.

Self-esteem is thinking well of oneself, liking oneself. One's self-esteem is not always explicit reflection of one's status in the world. More often it is based on how one *feels* about oneself, manifesting itself in the confidence with which one acts and talks and relates to other people. Self-esteem is a self-conscious quality, of course, and by self-consciousness we do not mean the rather sophisticated philosophical activity called reflection but the very ordinary experience of suddenly "catching oneself in the act." One can be wrong about whether he or she has high or low self-esteem and, as other people will be quick to detect, people with unacknowledged low self-esteem often act inconsiderate and arrogant by way of compensation. One's self-esteem may be tied to certain criteria of achievement or merit, but some people who have accomplished a great deal lack self-esteem, and some people who have accomplished very little sometimes seem full of it.

Self-respect is based on one's place in a community. It is a matter of social standing and a reflection of what other people think of us. But it is also a matter of how we think of ourselves. Thus the glutton is typically said to have no self-respect, not just because of what other people think of him but because he thinks so ill of himself. We recognize lack of self-respect in a person who goes to an important meeting unshaven or slovenly dressed, or gives a lecture unprepared, or talks about his sexual problems in a public forum. The public and the personal are not entirely separate spheres of life, of course, and so self-esteem and self-respect overlap all the time. Accomplishment alone is not enough to guarantee either of them. In fact, a firm place in a warm community is usually enough to maintain both self-respect and self-esteem. In the absence of such a community a lifetime of achievement may not suffice.

A Different Voice: Caring, Compassion, Love, and Friendship

Aristotle defends the essential role of reason in happiness and the good life, but he gives equal attention to the importance of having the right perceptions, emotions, impulses, and desires. Many of these feelings have to do with friendship and fellow-feeling, the bonds that hold us together not because of prudence or obligation or even as a means to happiness but just because we are social animals. We care for one another. We live in families and communities not because we have to but because we want to. "No one would choose to live without friends," insists Aristotle in his *Ethics,* and nearly a fifth of that book is devoted to the nature of friendship as an essential part of the good life. So, too, Plato devoted one of his best-known dialogues to the subject of *eros,* or love. The virtues of affection and fellow-feeling were essential virtues for the Greeks. To be happy and to be virtuous one needed to care about people and be cared about in turn. One needed friends and a family, love and affection. To be sure, the residual warrior mentality of the Greek philosophers did not allow them to express sentimentality about such subjects, but such feelings constituted an important part of Greek life, Greek ethics, and the Greek concept of the admirable person.

By contrast, what has struck many critics about modern ethics is the neglect and even contempt displayed for personal emotions. Deontologists such as Kant do not necessarily disdain the passions; they just dismiss them from the realm of practical reason. Kant had many friends, and according to personal accounts he was a warm and friendly person. But in an infamous passage on loving thy neighbor, Kant sarcastically remarks that such love must be commanded by reason as a duty and cannot be the "pathological" love of "melting compassion" (although *pathological* in this context means mainly "of the passions" rather than diseased). The general tendency of much modern ethics has been to consider the emotions, where they are not seen as a threat to rational thinking and dispassionate judgment, as pleasant or painful experiences to be calculated under the utilitarian accounting procedure. And while most of modern ethics puts a great deal of emphasis on personal morality and the public interest, relatively few ethicists spend much time talking about the more limited relationships that exist between two or just a few people, about friendship, the family, or love.

One of the aims of virtue ethics is to reintroduce the emotions and intimate personal relationships into ethics and our consideration of character. This interest in the emotions is not unique to modern times. In the eighteenth century, a group of virtue ethicists including David Hume his friend Adam Smith (who wrote *Wealth of Nations*, the bible of capitalism) defended an ethics of the "moral sentiments," in which feelings such as sympathy and compassion provided the foundation of all of ethics. Jean-Jacques Rousseau, another friend of Hume's, defended a theory of the natural sentiments as well. But perhaps the most powerful impetus behind this movement today comes from a number of feminist authors, who have insisted that the history of ethics has been dominated by men who have presented a distinctively male ethic of rational principles as if it were the whole of ethics. In an important book titled *A Different Voice* (1982), Carol Gilligan, a professor of educational psychology at Harvard, suggests that women tend to think about ethics primarily in terms of personal attachments and relationships, not in terms of abstract principles of obligation, as she says men do. She was specifically attacking a colleague of hers at Harvard, the psychologist Lawrence Kohlberg, who had long suggested that a Kantian-type deontological conception of ethics was the only fully mature conception. According to this view, young boys reached ethical maturity at a rather young age, while young girls seemed to get stuck at an earlier, less mature stage of moral development. Gilligan, in reply, argued that the paths of moral development were different, not the same, and the very nature of fully developed ethical values was quite different in men and women. The argument concerning moral development presupposed an important philosophical claim, namely that there were at least two different kinds of ethics, and some feminists began to argue for the superiority of the feminine ethic of caring. For example, Nell Noddings argues, in a book called *Caring*:

> One of the saddest features of this picture of violence [in the world today] is that the deeds are so often done in the name of principle. . . . This approach through law and principle is not, I suggest, the approach of the mother. It is the approach of the detached one, of the other. The view to be expressed here is a feminine view. . . . It is feminine in the deep classical sense—rooted in receptivity, relatedness, and responsiveness.

Feminist ethics has become one of the most important influences in ethics today. It finds a natural ally in virtue ethics, although, to be sure, there are as many different versions of feminist ethics as there are of virtue ethics, and only some of them are truly congruent with virtue ethics. The feminist argument reminds us of the important role of the moral sentiments and close and intimate relationships in happiness and the good life. It suggests that dispassionate reason (what some psycho-analysts would call dissociation) need not be seen as the highest virtue and insists that an admirable person will also be a passionate person who is concerned about other people and cares deeply about his or her family and loved ones. Hume, Rousseau, and Aristotle all believed that such personal attachments are of ultimate importance. Sympathy for strangers and a broader moral outlook are possible only as projections or extensions of such personal concern. What makes us moral, first of all, is our personal concern for those closest to us. Secondarily we learn to have similar concerns, even if based on principles rather than per-sonal attachments, for the many people we have never met and for hu-manity in general.

Hume, Smith, and Rousseau all describe the moral sentiments as natural. These sentiments are unlearned and they exist in everyone, al-though they can be destroyed by the wrong upbringing or, according to Rousseau, by the "corruption" of competitive society. The sentiment of *compassion,* literally "feeling with," is the most basic of our social feelings, according to these authors; it is the basis of all morality and the emotional glue that holds society and, ultimately, all humanity together. But the im-portance of compassion in ethics goes beyond its power to motivate gener-ous and helpful actions. The existence of compassion suggests that the harsh dichotomy between morality and selfishness may be a spurious one. Compassion, as an emotion, clearly has the power to move us. Indeed, we often act out of compassion without thinking about our behavior at all, leaping to another person's aid on impulse or feeling sorry for someone even before we understand what is wrong. But the point of compassion is always another being's interests and well-being, not one's own. Thus, at least some of our most spontaneous behavior is not in any way selfish. It is concerned with another person's well-being and therefore is an aspect of morality, not merely a personal impulse.

Compassion, according to Hume and Rousseau, is a sentiment that we feel toward any other person or creature, whether he or she or it is a member of our family or the family pet, a personal friend or a complete stranger. We can feel compassion for any person or creature in pain. But some of the moral sentiments are not so broad; they are very particular, sometimes even exclusive. A parent's love for her or his child or children is such a sentiment. Such love might in some rare instance be generalized to include all children, but usually it is restricted to one's own children. Friendship is a variety of love. The Greeks called it *philia,* in contrast to *eros* which is more like what we call romantic love. Friendship, too, is essential to ethics and the good life, and it is shocking how it has been left out of a great many moral theories or merely confined to the margins. When Aristotle insisted that no one would want to live without friends, he was not just projecting his own personal dependency. He was stating what he took to be a basic law of human nature and an indispensable component of both virtue and happiness. Friendship, too, is exclusive or, at least, restrictive. It is possible for a person to feel friendly toward almost everybody, but for most people one's true friends are few in number; they are a small, select group whom one knows and cares about most. Love is even more specialized than friendship, often limited to members of one's own family or intimate group, and romantic love is an emotion often described by its limitation to one and only one person, as exemplified in the social institution of marriage. If love and friendship are virtues, they stand opposed to all of those conceptions of morality that insist on the centrality of general principles and universalizability. The moral principle "Do not lie" applies equally to everyone and to every situation. The virtue of love may be restricted to a single individual.

One variety of love, sometimes called *agape* or "Christian love," is sometimes said to apply to everyone everywhere, without discrimination. It is the emotion commanded in the New Testament by Saint Paul, and it is the love that is sometimes equated with God. This love is not just a spontaneous feeling, which one may or may not have. It is a commandment, an obligation. Thus we can sense the curious conceptual trouble that Kant feels when he worries about whether the command "Love thy neighbor" (Matthew 22:39) should be considered a moral command, or a categorical imperative. If love is an emotion, he maintains, then it cannot be commanded, for it is not rational and not a matter of will. So such a command must be a matter of reason, and not an expression of the emotion love. In more ordinary terms, what bothers Kant is the idea that we can *love* everyone; we can have respect for everyone, but love, passionate love, is quite another matter.

The idea that ethics and morality should be based on love, and that love is the basis of the good life, has of course been at the center of human thinking for centuries. It is central to the ethics of the New Testament, and it is central to the religions of Judaism, Christianity, and Islam and many eastern religions as well. Hundreds of years ago, the troubadours crooned the virtues of love in France, and in the 1960s the Beatles sold several million copies of a song called "All You Need Is Love." The ethics of love is often equated with Christianity, but it is clearly defensible without religion; indeed, many of its most prominent defenders in recent years have not been religious at all. In any case, the ethics of love, whether expressed in the Bible or in New Age philosophy, is an insistence that fellow-feeling is primary in ethics. Rules and principles should be invoked only if necessary, when love has reached its limits.

Love and friendship do have their limits, as does compassion. It is almost impossible not to feel compassion for the handicapped child living next door or a single hungry child depicted in close-up in a magazine, but our reaction to the suffering of not a few but hundreds or thousands of people, who are located on the other side of the world, is seldom as acute. When we are dealing with people we don't know or may not like or with large numbers of people, it is clear that we need some guide beyond our feelings. Aristotle said that we need justice, a key virtue and an essential ingredient in morality, precisely when friendship and personal concern ends. Two thousand years later, Hume complained that our sense of sympathy becomes more and more diluted when those who are suffering are farther and farther away or exist in large numbers. He too argued for the importance of what he called an artificial, calculated virtue—justice. Justice, one could argue, is the natural extension of our care and concern for other people, from the realm of personal relationships and acquaintances to the larger realms of society, humanity, and perhaps life itself.

The Virtue of Community: Justice, Equality, Rights, and the Social Contract

Not only individuals, but communities too have virtues. Foremost among these, perhaps, is the virtue of justice. A good community will also be safe, friendly, and cooperative, and have many other virtues that make it both desirable to live in and desirable to live with, but justice has typically been singled out, from Plato and Aristotle to the recent work of Harvard philosopher John Rawls, as the crucial virtue of any community, institution, or society. Communities have often been described as extended families, and, indeed, in many societies they are extended families. Jean-Jacques Rousseau, in particular, suggested that the family is the initial model for any society. But as communities grow and expand they lose the sense of personal intimacy and interaction, and emotional attachments such as compassion, friendship, and personal affection are stretched thin. One might be expected to be generous and fair to one's friends and those whom one loves just because that is an essential part of friendship and love. But one cannot be so directly connected or concerned with the millions of people in his or her own country, much less with the several billion people in the world. And so our spontaneous feelings of community, compassion, love, and friendship have to be supplemented with a more abstract virtue, the virtue of justice.

Justice is often distinguished as having two forms: retributive justice and distributive justice. *Retributive justice* is essentially concerned with punishments, with assigning blame and punishing people in proportion to their misdeeds. *Distributive justice,* on the other hand, is concerned with the distribution of the goods of society, in part as a matter of reward but also in accordance with need and a number of other factors. The two kinds of justice are often treated independently, but they share common structures and concepts, in particular the concept of fairness and the importance of the notion of *equality.* Retributive justice is based on the idea that everyone should be treated fairly and as equal before the law. A poor man is not to be punished more harshly than a rich man, and two people who are imprisoned for exactly the same crime should receive similar sentences as well. In distributive justice a person is rewarded in accordance with what he or she deserves, and two people doing the same job equally well deserve the same compensation. To treat people unequally for irrelevant reasons—to punish a man or pay him less because of his race, for example—is a flagrant violation of justice. Fairness and equality thus become the central features of justice and the source of its most difficult problems too.

What is fair, and how do we know? To begin with, we can look at cases of *injustice:* a father who receives the death sentence for stealing a loaf of bread for his starving children, the innocent student who is singled out for punishment as an example for the entire class, the incompetent worker who receives a huge raise because she is the boss's niece. In each example we can begin to formulate reasons for thinking, here is a case of unfairness: In the first case we feel the punishment should fit the crime and extenuating circumstances should be considered. In the second we feel that blame should be restricted to those who actually did something wrong. No matter how effective making an example of an innocent student may be in deterring others, we feel that it is unfair to punish someone for something he or she didn't do. In the third case, we feel quite strongly that a person should get a reward only after earning it, and that being the boss's niece does not entitle one to special treatment.

The notion of fairness does not provide much of a definition of justice, if only because we so often use the words fairness and justice interchangeably. But fairness, in general, points to an agreeable fit between rewards and punishments and right and wrong actions. To break the agreed-upon rules of a game is unfair; to break a promise is unfair too. To punish an innocent person is unfair, but so is a punishment that is much more serious than the crime, for example, a life-term prison sentence for going ten miles over the speed limit. A punishment that is much less severe than the crime is also unjust (although the criminal will rarely complain). In the area of distributive justice, the fact that anyone should starve in the streets in a generally prosperous country also strikes many people as a gross injustice, and for "the rich to get richer while the poor get poorer" is also a case of unfairness to many people who may nevertheless have no doubt about the virtue of "getting rich."

Theories of distributive justice, like theories of morality, tend to be influenced by politics and ideology, by religion, and by one's upbringing. Three primary theories of distributive justice are vigorously defended in the world today. The first insists on a radical *egalitarianism*, on treating everyone as equals. By this view, it is unfair that anyone should have more than anyone else, and it is the role of the ruling body of the society, in most cases the government, to redistribute the goods of society from the rich to the poor. Such egalitarianism is part of the world view of communism, although it has rarely been practiced as preached even by the most fervently communist governments. This idea of distributive justice was defended by Karl Marx in the mid-nineteenth century, and it continues to be the view of a large number of people around the world who would generally call themselves socialists. Socialism does not always embody the extreme view that no one should have more than anyone else, for it has become evident over the past half century or so that certain inequalities are essential if most people are to have an effective incentive to work and if governments are not to become so intrusive and oppressive that they interfere with every aspect of a citizen's life. Moreover, a young child in need of care and education or an elderly person in need of constant medical attention may need much more in the way of material resources than a healthy, self-sufficient adult. A person who develops social skills or who expends an extraordinary amount of effort or takes special risks may well expect extra benefits. Marx famously said, "From each according to [one's] abilities; to each according to [one's] needs."

But can radical egalitarianism be put into practice in any society as we know it now? Can we cultivate a citizenry that would be willing to do their best without the promise or possibility of reward? Or would the attempt to form such a society inevitably lead to the political oppression, inefficiency, and even instances of mass murder seen in several twentieth-century communist regimes? In defense of the socialist theory of justice, it can be said that most of the governments that have claimed to adopt such a theory have paid little attention to justice and have only used the theory to enforce the state's political power. And the theory need not prohibit all inequalities, all personal ambitions, or all ungoverned initiatives. It need only insist poverty and deprivation in a land of plenty is intolerable and it is the obligation of the wealthy to eliminate that poverty and deprivation, by law if necessary. The central idea is that equality is the norm and deviations from the norm must have some special justification. Excessive deviations great wealth or poverty, should be corrected through the redistribution of wealth.

In direct contrast to such views, the *libertarian* view of justice rejects the idea of the redistribution of wealth, and is willing to accept inequalities as unavoidable. In this view, governments cannot step in and take away one person's goods in order to benefit another without violating that person's **rights.** It does not matter how needy the second person may be or how great the gap may be between the wealth of one and the poverty of the other. What is central to the libertarian theory of justice is the insistence that certain rights are inviolable, in particular the right to own and hold onto one's property. Theory also insists that such ownership must be legitimate, and so it permits the government to take away ill-gotten gains and give them back to their rightful owner. Indeed, such government power is itself legitimate and necessary just in order to protect property rights. The question of legitimate ownership, however, can become something of a muddle. If one's family home was stolen seven generations ago from the original natives of the region, does one have legitimate ownership? And if most of the civilized land on the earth was taken by force and perhaps more than once from its original inhabitants, can the notion of legitimate ownership even be made intelligible? Nevertheless, on a smaller scale, with everyday issues such as taxation and welfare, which are forms of government redistribution of wealth, the libertarian stance is quite clear: the government has no right to take from some citizens to give to others. The libertarian need not be devoid of compassion for the poor and, indeed, one of the corollaries of some libertarian theories is that those who are well off have an obligation, whether from a sense of Christian charity or noblesse oblige, to help those much worse off than themselves. What the libertarian objects to is being forced to do so.

As socialists become more tolerant of differences in wealth based on individual initiative and talent and libertarians become more concerned with the condition of the disadvantaged in society, we can start to see a middle ground, a theory that takes seriously both the importance of equality and the notion of rights. The best known of such *liberal* theories today is the theory of justice developed by John Rawls in his book *A Theory of Justice* (1971). Rawls defends two basic principles:

1. The equality principle: "Each person engaged in an institution or affected by it has an equal right to the most extensive liberty compatible with a like liberty for all."
2. The difference principle: "Inequalities as defined by the institutional structure or fostered by it are arbitrary unless it is reasonable to expect that they will work out to everyone's advantage and provided that the positions and offices to which they attach or from which they may be gained are open to all."

In Rawls's view, inequities are inevitable in society but there is a rational way of justifying them. An inequality must benefit everyone, not only the person who has a special advantage but especially the people who are the least advantaged. Thus it would be fair to allow some people to make fortunes from investments because, even if their doing so makes them much wealthier than everyone else, it also supports industry and improves the quality of life for everyone. But Rawls is no utilitarian. Indeed, we saw in part 2 that the utilitarian has a difficult time defending the theory against the accusation that it provides no grounds for considerations of justice, as when an act that maximizes utility does so by violating the rights of some individual or small group of individuals. Furthermore, utility may be maximized in the face of extreme inequality and injustice, as when some undeserving people become very very rich and others who may be much more deserving remain poor. Rawls takes the view of the deontologist. He develops his principles on strictly rational grounds. He does not make a plea for compassion or an appeal to personal self-interest. Like Kant, he appeals to any rational agent on grounds of reason alone.

In defending his theory of justice Rawls invokes a general conception of justice that is shared by a great many ethicists and most Americans. It is the idea, derived in part from Kant's notion of autonomy, that people have the right to make agreements with one another, and these agreements are then binding on them. The simplest example is the making of a promise, such as making a commitment to pay back a loan or show up for a recital or keep a secret. A more formal example of such an agreement is a *contract*, in which you explicitly commit yourself to certain actions in the future, presumably in return for some reciprocal action on the part of the other parties to the contract. Such agreements and contracts have a special place in our view of ethics. It is one thing to be forced or fooled or cajoled into performing a certain action or behaving in a certain way, the way a young child might be cowered or tricked into behaving well for a new babysitter. But such manipulation smacks of paternalism, and while it may be excusable or necessary for parents to use such control with young children, it is generally considered demeaning and inappropriate for adults. Adults like to think that they do what they do because they themselves chose to do it, and in much of morality and social life they like to think that they behave in a proper and ethical way not just because they were raised to do so but also because they, as well as everyone else, has agreed to do so. It is as if, according to this widespread and popular view, everyone in the society had signed a contract and formed an agreement. The people agree to principles such as, "I will not cheat or threaten you if you do not cheat and threaten me," and so on. Of course, such agreements need not be formalized in a written contract, as in the Constitution of the United States, but they are implied in everything that we do. In either case a *social contract* exists, and it is, according to many ethicists, the key to our concept of justice.

In the seventeenth century the English philosopher Thomas Hobbes proposed a social contract theory of human society. Hobbes was a radical thinker who, like so many philosophers, got in serious trouble for his ideas. In particular, he challenged the age-old and obviously self-serving doctrine of the divine right of kings. For Hobbes, the king ruled by agreement with his people, because he was necessary to hold society together, not because he was anointed by God. Hobbes suggests that, in the "state of nature," before people joined together in society, they lived in a state of constant war of everyone against everyone. Life, he says, was "nasty, brutish and short." And so people came together and agreed to a social contract, in which each person agreed to leave the others alone and give up certain rights to the king, or sovereign.

Life became more peaceful, but the most valuable result of the social contract, according to Hobbes, was the concept of justice. There was no justice in the state of nature, only force and physical power. But in the web of agreements that tied men and women together in society, justice became the name for their mutual obligations and expectations. Years later, John Locke developed a similar model of the social contract, which became one of the bases of the American Constitution, and Jean-Jacques Rousseau developed another version of the social contract in which he claims that everyone ultimately imposes the law on himself or herself, rather than be forced by society to submit to its dictates. It is this idea of our imposing the law on ourselves, that is, choosing and agreeing to the rules by which we will live, that makes the social contract view of justice so appealing. The social contract model establishes the foundation of justice in mutual agreement. The principles of justice are not imposed on us by society; we have chosen them ourselves.

Rawls adopts the model of the social contract and asks us to imagine that we are in the odd but somewhat spectacular position of preparing to set up a society in which we ourselves will have to live. In this situation the danger exists that we will each introduce self-interested suggestions. For example, if I am intelligent, I might suggest that intelligent people and jobs that require intelligence be richly rewarded. A man might well insist that men should have the better jobs than women or get higher pay. A chronically ill person might insist that special care and attention be paid to the ill, while a young, healthy person might make no provisions for the sick or the elderly at all. To neutralize such biases, Rawls suggests that we assume that we do not know what our position will be in society, whether we will be sick or healthy, intelligent or chronically retarded, male or female. We do not know whether we will be born into a family with wealth or a family in poverty, into a neighborhood that is safe and secure or a slum in which life is unsafe and insecure. And so we make our choices in a state of uncertainty. Since we do not know whether we will suffer some serious, debilitating illness or not, we would probably design a society in which people who develop or are born with such illnesses are taken care of. Since we do not know whether we will be born rich or poor, we would likely arrange society so that no one will have to suffer extreme poverty. Thus we all must be rational, at least in the sense that we cannot pursue what we know to be our own self-interests but must take into account the interests of everyone.

Even given the uncertainty of our future position in such a planned society, some people might be willing to take their chances, hoping that with luck they will be born healthy and wealthy and at least intelligent enough to make their mark in the world. But most people, Rawls surmises, would rather play it safe, and so they will minimize risk by designing a society that is as equal as possible. Most rational planners will design a society in which everyone has optimum opportunity whatever the circumstances of their birth and in which those who are most disadvantaged will benefit from the society too. For example, we might very well be willing to give some people more power than others so that they can form a government, on the grounds that everyone will benefit from an orderly society (almost everyone would suffer in a society where there is equality but universal chaos). And we would very likely be willing to give that government the power to redistribute wealth, just in case we find ourselves one of the very poor. But in the interests of prosperity, we would probably also agree to a system of rewards that encourages people to work as hard as possible, thus benefiting the entire society as well as themselves. They may become wealthier and more powerful than everyone else, but the benefits that they produce for the rest of society make this inequality more than tolerable.

Thus equality remains the ideal, but it is offset by the recognition that inequalities may, within certain limits, be of considerable benefit to everyone.

We are still left with the question, What is equality? A belief in equality is not the claim that everyone is naturally endowed with the same abilities and talents. Some people are born with intelligence, while others are not. Some people are born healthy while others are sickly or crippled for life. Some people are reared in loving homes with good examples of happiness all around them. Others are raised in miserable circumstances. It is also not the claim that everyone makes equally valuable contributions to society. A student who works his or her way through the local night school with mediocre grades because of having to work all day may never be in a position to make the dramatic contributions to society possible for the well-bred Harvard graduate who through family and friends has political connections and power. We might say that both of these students make contributions to the best of his or her ability, but we would probably not say the contributions are equal in impact.

In the arena of education, at least in a democratic society, the issue of equality seems to turn on the idea of equal opportunity. But this concept is also an elusive one. Is there any sense in giving two children the same educational opportunities when one, with proper training, will obviously learn a great deal, while the other, even with an exhausting effort, will learn very little? Of course, we could be wrong about their potential. A bright child may never fulfill his or her promise, and the slow student in back of the class occasionally emerges as a great scholar or scientist. We could say that all students deserve equal opportunity, but since even very young students enter school with very different abilities and backgrounds, this cannot mean simply that everyone should receive exactly the same education. The problem with treating everyone equally is that the best students will be unchallenged while the poorest students may be left behind. We might insist that each student should be educated to maximize his or her potential for the good of both self and society. But if we do not have the resources for such an educational program, how should we make our choices? Some students begin with considerable educational advantages. Should they be given special consideration, at the expense of everyone else? Some students begin with severe educational disadvantages. Should they be given special attention, at the expense of everyone else? If the worst students cannot utilize the same opportunities as the best students, should the better students therefore be penalized? In a short story the writer Kurt Vonnegut describes a society with an intricate system of handicaps—to make strong people weaker, graceful people clumsy, beautiful people plain, and smart people distracted—all in the name of equality. Many recent political thinkers, too, have objected that the emphasis on equality in modern society can have the disastrous consequence of encouraging mediocrity.

It has proven to be very difficult to formulate a notion of equality that is not hopelessly vague and that will do the important political work we want it to do. Nevertheless, some notion of equality is essential to justice, to ensure that people are given equal opportunities for advancement and the good life and are punished similarly by the law for the crimes they commit. But equality is not the only important aspect of our notion of justice, even in our unusually egalitarian society. We also insist that people get what they deserve—punishment for their crimes, rewards for their contributions—and in this sense we insist on treating people unequally. We summarize this aspect of justice with the word *merit.* Because people make different contributions, they deserve different rewards from society. Even if people do not succeed in their endeavors, we feel they should be rewarded for their effort (or punished for the lack of it). We also believe that people should be rewarded for setting an example, whether or not they personally produce anything as such, and that people in positions of responsibility deserve extraordinary reward, just by virtue of their visibility and accountability. Sometimes, we are willing to reward people extravagantly just because they are popular and command a sizable share of the mass market for entertainment. We also believe that people should be rewarded, sometimes extravagantly, for taking risks, for example, when they invest money in a new product or a new company.

Another aspect of justice is the notion of *entitlement.* Central to the libertarian view is the importance of the concept of rights. People have a right to keep what the earn and use what they own, and to interfere with this right is an injustice. Justice entitles people to certain goods, perhaps because they have worked and earned them, but perhaps even if they have not earned them in any way. If a dying parent gives everything away to his or her child or to an old college roommate, that is a private decision and, no matter how deserving, the child or the roommate is thereby entitled to the inheritance. Of course, one might object to the advantages and abuses of inheritance, but our sense of justice clearly includes some sense of entitlement.

Finally, justice requires that those who cannot care for themselves be cared for. We believe this whether or not we are prepared to defend the general Marxist conception of justice, to each according to his or her needs. It is not just compassion or charity that prompts us to help those who are without family and financial support. There are levels of deprivation and inequality that no civilized society can or should tolerate. In any considerations of distributive justice, this is the bottom line: no one should be left with nothing.

Next to equality, the concept of rights is probably the most important aspect of justice. The libertarian invokes the concept of property rights to ward off government taxation and the redistribution of property. He or she may also invoke the concept of individual rights to prevent the government from interfering with freedom of speech, the practice of religion, or any number of personal activities that might be classified under the general heading, "the pursuit of happiness." Marxists and other socialists invoke the right of everyone to a decent job, adequate housing, and a reasonable standard of life. So do liberals, although they do not necessarily insist that it is the government's responsibility to provide these. Rawls mentions the right to liberty in his first principle (see page 141). Thus rights are virtually as important as the concept of justice itself.

A *right* is first of all a claim, a demand of sorts, which is made by one person on another, or on an entire society. Every right thus has a corresponding obligation. For example, every person in our society has a constitutionally guaranteed right to freedom of speech, which means that everyone else (as well as the government) has the obligation not to infringe upon that right. Many people insist that every member of our society has a right to a decent job and a good education, although these are not guaranteed by the Constitution. The libertarian would quickly insist that it is not just or fair to provide jobs and education for everyone if that involves violating the rights of some to improve the lot of others. This idea of obligation is at the heart of some of the most heated battles concerning justice in our society. Should some people be forced to help others, even when we acknowledge that some sort of help is necessary?

There are different kinds of rights. Some rights, such as those guaranteed by the Constitution or other laws of the land, are *legal rights*, rights by virtue of the law. Such rights, however, are clearly relative to a particular society and its laws. A man has a right to marry many wives in some societies, not in others. A woman has the right to vote in some societies, not in others. But we would not want to say that the rights guaranteed by our Constitution, in particular, are rights *merely* by virtue of the law. Rather, we would say that they are rights essential to society, whether or not they are canonized in law. Rights that are essential to the nature of a certain society are often called *civil rights*. Basic aspects of our society such as the belief in equality, for example, are manifested in such civil rights as the right not to be discriminated against because of race or religion or sex. Not surprisingly, civil rights are typically written into law, and thus become legal rights as well.

Although civil rights are relative to the customs of a particular society, some of these rights seem to deserve universal status as principles of morality. These are called *human rights* or *natural rights* because they apply to all human beings everywhere, regardless of the customs of their particular societies. For example, the right not to be tortured is generally agreed to be such a right. It does not matter whether it is written into law or part of the culture of a society; torture is a violation of human rights. So too, according to the United Nations Declaration of 1948, every person on earth has the human right to "social security . . . and a standard of living adequate for health and well-being." Notice that this last example introduces a different notion of right, based on need. Indeed, one way to categorize all rights, from the most basic human rights to the most specific and sometimes trivial legal rights, such as the right of high school students to wear jeans to class, is into freedom rights and entitlement rights. *Freedom rights* (or negative rights) are rights not to be interfered with, to be left alone. The right to freedom of speech, the right to privacy, the right to worship as one chooses, the right to choose one's friends and travel where one wishes—these are all freedom rights, in which other people and the government are obliged to leave us alone. *Entitlement rights* (or positive rights) are those that allow a person to make a legitimate claim to goods that other people have to provide. Entitlement rights could include the right to medical care, the right to a decent job, the right to decent housing, and the right to an adequate education. These are sometimes viewed as promises made by the society in its social contract to each and every individual within it. But it is important to remember that the same contract that promises certain benefits extracts in return a number of obligations. We may be entitled to certain goods and services from society, but society is entitled to certain goods and services from us as well. In wartime those services may even include giving up one's life.

The concept of rights is often and easily abused. We see in our society a disturbing proliferation of rights claims. We agree that a person has the right to freedom of speech. Does that include the freedom to burn the American flag or desecrate other people's churches or religious symbols? We have the right to protect ourselves. Does that right entitle a private citizen to own a weapon manufactured for the purpose of blowing up enemy tanks or shooting airplanes out of the sky? We count these rights as part of the right to pursue our own happiness. But because we are so used to freedom in so many aspects of life, we tend to think that we have the right not to be interfered with in any instance, no matter how disruptive or obnoxious or even dangerous we may be. Rights have to be balanced against the other components of justice, including the public good and the well-being of others. Our rights may be precious, but they are but one aspect of a grand moral virtue of justice that encompasses all of society.

Virtue versus Morality: A Radical View

While we have seen that virtue ethics is compatible with the modern moral philosophies of Kant and Mill, and can expand and enhance traditional moral theory, some exponents of virtue ethics would have virtue ethics replace the traditional considerations of morality. One of the most radical advocates of virtue ethics is the German philosopher Friedrich Nietzsche. Nietzsche did not defend virtue ethics as a complement to morality. He used virtue ethics as a weapon to attack the very idea of morality. Nietzsche is often called a *nihilist* because of his uncompromising rejection of morality, but Nietzsche was no nihilist. He did not reject ethics as such, nor did he (usually) insist that everyone has his or her own values. Indeed, his argument against morality was first of all that it forced people to share the same values, without regard to their individual talents, virtues, or differences. Furthermore, the values they shared were typically of a pathetic variety, notably, the pursuit of pleasure and security. Nietzsche thus rejected the abstract, universal rules of the Kantians as well as what he considered the vulgar emphasis on pleasure and utility of the utilitarians. He focused instead, as Aristotle had long before him, on the exceptional character, the great-souled person who rises above the hoi poloi, or herd. Nietzsche praises the more than human hero who passionately pursues his or her own way, whether or not this accords with the system of principles and prohibitions called morality. In fact, Nietzsche's attack on morality is not so much an attack on the substance of moral principles as an attack on the very idea of universal principles and the timid, herdlike motives of those who act according to them. But behind his rhetoric, we might note, Nietzsche believed in keeping his promises and being a good neighbor. He did not believe in hurting people, and one of his last acts in life was to save a horse from a beating. What he did believe was that at least some people could make themselves better than the rest, and the idea of morality, rather than improving them, made them simply mediocre and ordinary, not admirable or exceptional at all.

The Kantian emphasis on intentions presumes proper motives lie behind our actions. But what if the motives behind even our most exemplary moral behavior were in fact selfish or self-interested, as the psychological egoist might argue? What if our most altruistic intentions were rather a devious strategy for winning others' approval or gaining an advantage over them? Even Kant admits (a century before Freud) that we may not be conscious of all of the motives of our actions. He only insists that the moral worth for our actions must be measured according to those quite conscious intentions involved in acting on principle. His emphasis, understandably, is on those worthy intentions, such as wanting to do one's duty and showing respect for the law. So, too, philosophers who would rather emphasize emotions and other inclinations that motivate our behavior, such as David Hume, emphasize our more benign feelings, such as sympathy, love, and fellow-feeling. But suppose the springs of action were not so noble and the motives for morality were not so much concerned with duty, compassion, and fellow-feeling.

Suppose even the most benign feelings were really a front for hostility, competitiveness, or timidity (as biologists have suggested that the human smile originated as a sign of submission)? Suppose the dominant motive for morality was not the desire to do one's duty but rather fear or some other pathetic emotion. What would we say about morality then? Would we still feel, as we now do, that morality ought to have trump status among our various rules and principles?

This drastic challenge to morality has always been around. Socrates had to argue against it in the early books of Plato's *Republic,* and Saint Augustine was painfully aware of its possibility. But the thinker who is most responsible for elevating this suspicion about morality to a full-blown philosophy is Nietzsche. Morality, he argues, is not motivated by duty or respect or love or sympathy. It is motivated by fear, envy, and resentment. Much of traditional morality, he points out, has been motivated by the hardly honorable emotion of sheer terror—of one's masters, of the king, and, most of all, of God. Millions may have walked the straight and narrow in order to avoid the everlasting flames of Hell, but that scarcely entitles them to any claim to nobility. Action for the sake of duty may be honorable, even admirable, Nietzsche would maintain, but action based only on fear is timidity or at best prudence, not virtue.

Not only fear but the vicious emotions of envy and resentment are motives for morality, according to Nietzsche. Indeed, Nietzsche sometimes characterizes morality itself as "the greatest act of revenge in history." Revenge for whom? And against whom? Nietzsche tells us that it is the revenge of the weak against the strong, of the losers against the winners, of the slaves against their masters. Thus Nietzsche distinguishes between "master morality" and "slave morality." *Master morality* is an ethics of virtue and excellence. It applies only to the best and most admirable people. Slave morality—what in contemporary parlance and Kant's philosophy would simply be called morality—is a reactionary value system that rejects the virtues of the powerful and privileged and substitutes for them ordinary virtues, meekness in place of strength, humility in place of pride, innocence in place of experience, ignorance in place of wisdom, and so on. The commandments of ordinary morality, according to Nietzsche, are meant to discourage the virtues of the most exemplary members of society and to encourage the timid mediocrity of the untalented, the uncreative, the powerless.

Morality thus consists of prohibitions against the strong for the protection and edification of the weak. Why else, Nietzsche suggests, would so many of our moral principles be negative, beginning with "Thou shalt not . . ."? How else can one interpret such promises as "The meek shall inherit the earth" and "It is easier for a camel to pass through the eye of a needle than for a rich man to enter the Kingdom of Heaven"? These are the expressions of envy and resentment, the bitterness of those who do not have power, wealth, and earthly glory against those who do have them. Morality, Nietzsche concludes, is not the noble aspect of our lives that we have pretended. It is an expression of weakness and therefore ignoble and hypocritical, pretending to be something that it is not. Morality is a diabolically clever strategy invented by the weaker and more impoverished members of society to protect themselves from the stronger and more powerful. It restricts the ambitions and curbs the desires of those who would be superior and transgress the rules that enforce civil behavior and universal mutual respect. Universal principles are not a function of practical reason but a form of leveling, keeping the most talented and ambitious people down by pretending that everyone is really the same. Morality is thus the enemy of excellence. Not surprisingly, Nietzsche defends a "great man" theory of history, in which a society moves forward only through the actions of a handful of exceptional individuals—artists and thinkers as well as warriors and diplomats—and the well-being of the average citizen is of only secondary significance.

Nietzsche has inspired many readers with visions of greatness as well as entertained them with his biting wit and stinging critique of the hypocrisy and vacuousness of other moral theories. But while it is easy to be caught up in his dashing brilliance and the rousing encouragement to escape from the herd, we must insert a cautious note. What would it mean to create one's own virtues, as Nietzsche urges, and how would one go about doing it? And what if one is not, afterall, one of Nietzsche's exceptional heroes? Is it so bad to act out of fear, or even resentment, if one has reason to be prudent or is rightly offended or oppressed by others? What's wrong with pursuing security and happiness in the perfectly ordinary sense? Is it justifiable to put so much weight on individual character apart from any concern for the public good? Aristotle, who defended virtue ethics twenty-four centuries before Nietzsche, would have dismissed Nietzsche's reasoning. A virtue for him was an excellence that was publically defined and expressed in public performances, not a personal creation and perhaps a merely private sense of accomplishment. There is much to admire and even more to ponder in Nietzsche's attack on morality and defense of exceptional character, but it is a radicalism that should be read with caution, a strong medicine that should be measured by how much one can safely swallow.

Saints, Heroes, and Rogues

Nietzsche's point about the inadequacy of morality is one that has bothered traditional moralists, including such theorists as Kant and Mill, for some time. Much of what is discussed under the name of morality has to do with fulfilling obligations, or doing one's duty. But what one morally ought to do is limited, and much of morality consists of prohibitions rather than positive recommendations or ideals for action. Furthermore, as we have already noted, one problem with a conception of morality that is limited to obeying the rules is that a perfectly good person might also be a completely unexceptional person whose behavior benefits and inspires no one. When morality depends strictly on doing one's duty, morality itself becomes a dreary and quite boring affair. A self-proclaimed "immoralist," Nietzsche thus suggests that this type of morality is essentially a leveling device intended to lop off the peaks of human excellence as well as to raise up the herd to a higher form of behavior. But extraordinary behavior—heroic and saintly deeds—would be ignored in such a conception and, indeed, moral theorists in the Kantian mold have been hard pressed to give an adequate account of those who go far beyond their moral duties to display such extraordinary behavior. A special term has been invented for behavior that is "beyond the call of duty": *supererogatory*. Thus those exemplary acts and people that are at the very heart of ethics are converted into a curious and problematic set of exceptions.

We can better understand the nature of these inspiring examples in terms of virtue ethics than in terms of morality and obedience to principles. One of the most inspiring facts in ethics is that there are people who go far beyond the rules, not breaking them but far exceeding their demands. Thus the good man, for Aristotle, is not just one who obeys the rules but one who excels in what he does. This is not to say that he disobeys the rules and laws of Athenian society; he just does not often think of them because they are second nature. The good man is not only expected not to flee from battle but to fight to the best of his ability. He is not only expected not to lie (which is easy enough if you keep silent) but to be witty and clever and informative, if not as brilliant as Socrates. People have always had heroes. Today, perhaps, because of the mass media, there are more examples of personal excellence and exceptional virtue in which the pronouncement of principles plays but a small role. But such examples may be far more appealing and powerful than the abstractions of morality, and we may well want to agree with Nietzsche that the ethics of heroism is far more inspiring than the mundane world of morality.

This idea of going beyond morality, beyond the call of duty, is embodied best in those special people whom we designate as saints and heroes. A *saint* is not just someone who is perfectly good in the sense of not sinning (it is possible that the person has not had the opportunity to sin). A saint is extraordinarily good in that he or she resists temptations that we cannot imagine resisting and does good deeds that are far beyond the demands of duty or charity. Similarly, a *hero,* or *heroine,* is a person who does not do just what is commanded, but does much more than anyone could have expected. One cannot command saintliness or heroism, and it is no one's duty to be a saint or a hero or heroine. Nevertheless, our ethics would be impoverished without such models of behavior to inspire us to be our best. Refraining from a forbidden act because of fear of punishment or anticipation of guilt may still count as moral, but it is nothing like, and does not feel at all like, the sense of nobility that Aristotle and Nietzsche would say motivates our best actions. Acting from a sense of duty may be motivated and accompanied by a comforting sense of righteousness, but the saint or the hero typically does not even think of what they are doing in such terms. Indeed, it may be in part that naiveté, the absence of self-doubt and deliberation, that make a person a saint or a hero.

Saints and heroes have the virtues appropriate to their cultures. These will not, obviously, all be the same. The Christian saints had different virtues from those of the Buddha, and Saint Francis had different virtues from those of Mohammed. Achilles and Alexander the Great had very different virtues from those of Gandhi and Martin Luther King, and Einstein had a different set of virtues than Galileo. The virtues of the saints and heroes are not just the ordinary virtues that make a good person, such as honesty, trustworthiness, and a sense of humor. Indeed, their virtues may even eclipse some of those more ordinary virtues altogether, particularly in times of moral turmoil. A person who is extremely devout may lack a sense of humor. A person who is extremely successful in battle may have told lies to ensure that success.

The occasional conflict between the more ordinary virtues and the extraordinary virtues of saints and heroes highlights the ethical phenomenon of the *rogue.* Many familiar heroes and heroines in contemporary American literature and culture are rogues. The rogue is often a

stylish figure, played in movies by charming or seductive stars. Typically, the rogue breaks the law, or at least is at odds with the law, and
committing crimes outright is not unusual. In American movies, such
outlaw behavior might include the violation of no fewer than several
dozen traffic laws within a ten-minute chase scene. In literary criticism,
such a character is often called an *antihero,* a term that expresses some
ethical confusion about the fact that the person has the status but not
all of the morals of a hero.

Why should such a character be mentioned in ethics at all, except
perhaps as an unfortunate popular example of rampant immorality? Because, first of all, like it or not, these heroes and heroines provide moral
examples for millions of American children and teenagers, and one
would be dangerously mistaken in relegating such figures to the world
of mere entertainment. Second, such examples illustrate quite clearly
the complexity of our actual morals and moral conceptions, which are
not limited to universal rules and obedience but include an admiration
for those who dare to be different, so long as they are admirable or
exceptional in some appealing way. Third, they highlight the enormous
range of the concept of character in ethics.

It would be misleading, however, to leave the example of the rogue
in the hands of American moviemakers, as if the sole occupation of such
characters were the perpetration of financially rewarding felonies. There
is a history of far more honorable rogues, who have compensating virtues that go beyond superficial charm and attractiveness and provide rewards for society for generations to come. These rogues include many
of the great artists of past centuries who were famously difficult people
and often selfish and immoral as well. Whether they had to be so to be
great artists or became so because they were great artists, are two
much-discussed but dubious hypotheses which we need not explore
here. Beethoven scandalized most of Viennese society with his lack of
manners and untrustworthiness, and before him Mozart carried on in a
most improper manner. The great French author Balzac motivated him-

self to write by plunging deeply in debt with high living, and some of the greatest poets who followed him, such as Rimbaud and Baudelaire, led immoral lives in Paris. Picasso's moral eccentricities have been much publicized in recent years, but his behavior is not very different from that of a great many famous artists, male and female, in the bohemian culture in which the arts have flourished for the past century or so. In the realm of the intellect, Freud and Jung have often been accused of inconsiderate if not immoral behavior toward their psychoanalytic colleagues. Even Martin Luther has often been portrayed as a man who was deeply neurotic, frequently inconsistent if not hypocritical, and cruel to many of those closest to him. And yet, given the enormous contributions of these persons, it seems beside the point to dwell on their personal failings.

My point here is not to defend immorality. The behavior of rogues is rarely immoral in any repulsive sense. Otherwise, they would quickly lose their status as heroes of any kind. It is to show once again that our ethics is a complex and flexible system of concerns, as complex and as flexible as our pluralistic ethos. Indeed, one reason that the rogues are so important to us is that they often attack corrupt or unreasonable authority, stand up for the "little guy," and represent the oppressed minority against the dominant majority. Thus, despite their occasional immorality or criminality, the rogue represents some of the virtues most prized in our society—independence, humor, initiative, a kind of courage, and a deep concern for others—which go beyond mere rule-following. To think of the rogue as simply immoral, therefore, is to miss his or her ethical significance. And to focus on a single moral examplar who is guided only by duty is to paint an emaciated picture of ethics and present an inaccurate picture of our ethos.

Ethics, Ethos, and Pluralism: American Morality Today

Once upon a time, we like to imagine, morality was a simple matter and everyone agreed on what was right and what was wrong. In such an uncomplicated situation, the question of justification would have been unlikely, and the very idea of ethical relativism would have seemed absurd. It is unlikely, however, that there has ever been such a time. Every society, no matter how seemingly homogeneous, has produced its deviants, its doubters, its troublemakers. Sometimes such people have been simply ignored, or ridiculed, or isolated. Sometimes they have been tortured, or exiled, or killed. Throughout most of history, those who have questioned the ethics of their own culture have been condemned to silence, or worse. But today the world is a smaller place, and different cultures constantly mix and collide and at times their moralities as well as their national interests and religions come into conflict. Our own society is, if not a melting pot, a mixed salad, in which dozens of cultures coexist, many of them in the same city, on the same block, or in the same school or church. Mutual examination, criticism, and conflict are as inevitable as mutual tolerance is necessary. Given this diversity and contact, one is more likely than ever to question his or her own values, perceive and appreciate alternatives, and seek some justification for doing one thing rather than another, or embracing one value rather than another. Aristotle presented a picture of Athenian morality that was a unified, generally agreed-upon whole, with no need for justification and not even a bow to alternative moralities. This self-promoting image is misleading, however, as even a cursory glance at the history of his time and place shows. Aristotle's Greece was a cauldron of cultural conflicts, both within Greek society and between Greeks and the barbarians around them. In our own culture, the meeting ground for most of the cultures of the world, we acknowledge differences but still attempt to see a unified whole, using the term pluralism as if it were a single ethic to mask the cultural conflicts that frequently occur.

In recognizing the plurality of mores and morals by which we live, theories of ethics, especially in the United States, have tended toward *noncognitivism.* Noncognitivists deny that ethics is a matter of truth and falsehood, that one can justify a single correct moral position. But noncognitive theories are not just about the justification of morality; they are also as expressions of a particular ethical point of view. In his recent book *After Virtue,* Alasdair MacIntyre has analyzed emotivism and other noncognitive theories of morality as the expression of a culture which has all but lost sight of morality and its essential nature. It is as though some grave catastrophe had destroyed our whole language and practice of morality, MacIntyre suggests, and all that is left are a few scattered words like *ought* and *moral* and a debatable collection of principles whose point and purpose have been forgotten. Emotivism and other noncognitive theories, he hypothesizes, are not so much metaethical theories about the nature of ethics and its language as they are the philosophical expressions of a culture in which moral claims actually have lost their purpose, in which it is generally accepted that we will never agree on such basic ethical issues as the rightness of abortion, the justifiability of war, or the justice of taxation and the redistribution of wealth. If we compare this ethical conflict and confusion with the ethos that Aristotle at least claimed to find among his fellow Greeks, the difference is unsettling. Aristotle regularly appeals to the general agreement of his fellow citizens on critical moral issues, and the idea that ethical issues might be undecidable and a matter of mere personal opinion would have struck him and other Greeks as the most dangerous kind of utter nonsense.

What is missing in our ethics, in other words, is a sense of an ethos, an already established and agreed-upon way of living in which values are shared. But this may not be a tragedy, and it may well be that Aristotle was fooling himself. In any ethos one can justify and criticize principles and actions within the ethos, but what one cannot do is to try to stand outside one's ethos and evaluate or justify all of its values and principles at once. To do so leaves oneself without any basis whatsoever for making the evaluation or, insofar as it is possible to adopt the viewpoint of an alternative ethos, removes the perspective that made life in that ethos possible in the first place. The significant sentiments and emotional reactions a person has within his or her ethos are quite naturally be the cultivated products of one's upbringing, but outside of any ethos all sentiments and emotional reactions may seem merely accidental and unjustifiable. Even the dictates and principles of reason may be self-evident within an ethos but arbitrary and unprovable without it. Without an ethos, in other words, there is no basis for the justification of morals. Within an ethos, however, no ultimate justification may be possible or necessary. What is necessary but difficult is learning how to be both in and beyond our own ethos, and that is ethics today.

For MacIntyre our entire culture reflects the disintegration of the communal and cultural contexts within which morality and the virtues alone make sense. But this unsympathetic view of the dynamics of a pluralist society is overly pessimistic. Plato and Aristotle did not engage in the quest for justification that is central to modern ethics, but they, too, were trying to unify a divided society. Insofar as they did so, Nietzsche argues, it was because their Greek society too was already past its golden age and starting to decay. We can understand the uncompromising nature of their ethics if we recognize their vision of potential chaos in the background. When MacIntyre traces the quest for justification to the eighteenth-century and the Enlightenment, he claims that the European sense of ethos was already falling apart and the search for universal values and principles was taken up in earnest by way of compensation. But an alternative view is that during the Enlightenment the scope and breadth of humanity was for the first time being taken seriously into account; if the attempt at unity was clumsy and defensive, the enormity of the task is an adequate explanation. David Hume's rejection of the justification of morality was part of the ethical atmosphere of skepticism within which the quest for justification was being carried out, but he himself tried, in his theory of the moral sentiments, to tie all of humanity together by a bond of nature. Nietzsche, in MacIntyre's analysis, was simply the final, fatal blow to an already collapsing system of morality. But an alternative view is that Nietzsche was one of the first philosophers before the twentieth century to fully appreciate the importance of pluralism.

What MacIntyre suggests might too easily be mistaken for nostalgic despair and an impossible plea to return to a mythical past. "Forward to the twelfth century," he half-jokingly comments. But his criticism of the whole ethical tradition from Hume to Moore and the noncognitivists serves as a warning that our current polarized attitude toward ethics and the philosophical theories in which they are expressed may be a trap. We try too hard, and impossibly, to be above any particular society and culture and so, in the name of universalism, find ourselves nowhere at all. Or we insist on rationally justifying the moral principles of our ethos and end up wondering on what grounds if any we could condemn even a Hitler or a sadist. But ethics need not take the form of a rigid set of moral principles backed by an ironclad theory of justification. Rather it is a shared way of life in which certain practices and rules of morality play an accepted rule but are flexible and always open to question. To question everything is to be left with nothing, but to refuse to question at all, or to insist on an ultimate justification, relegates morality to the realm of stubborn habits and condemns multicultural society to bitter political and endless battles. But we will never find the security of the good life as long as we believe that we are swimming in a veritable sea of values without any hope of common agreement or that our group is right and everyone else is wrong.

What we need, therefore, is a new ethics of pluralism, an ethics especially suited to contemporary America rather than the ancient Greek polis or the small towns of Kant's eighteenth-century Germany. The naive and lazy relativist view that values are just a matter of personal opinion must be recognized as just as nonsensical and dangerous as the dogmatic view that one's own morals are absolutely correct and everyone else is wrong. We are not a society without values, much less a society in which every act is no better and no worse than any other. But we are a society with a multiplicity of values, in which it therefore becomes all the more urgent for each of us to clarify, understand, and, within modest limits, justify our values and our views. The ethé of many traditional societies are already established and in process of coming apart, but the complex ethos that constitutes American society is still in the making, and it is by doing ethics that we can assist in its formation.

Recommended Reading

Many of the classic texts discussed in this book are included, with commentary, in Solomon, *Morality and the Good Life,* 2nd ed. (New York: McGraw-Hill, 1991). The classic contemporary critique of traditional moral philosophy is Alasdair MacIntyre, *After Virtue* (Notre Dame, IN: Univ. of Notre Dame Press, 1981). An even harsher view is put forward by Richard Taylor in *Good and Evil* (Buffalo, NY: Prometheus Books, 1984). A good collection on various issues in virtue ethics is Peter French, ed., *Ethical Theory: Virtue and Character* (Notre Dame, IN: Univ. of Notre Dame Press, 1988). Two good short discussions of contemporary issues are Peter Singer, *Practical Ethics* (Cambridge: Cambridge Univ. Press, 1979) and James Rachels, *The Elements of Moral Philosophy* (New York: Random House, 1986). John Rawls's *Theory of Justice* (Cambridge, MA: Harvard Univ. Press, 1971) is a classic but very difficult reading for an introductory student. Some helpful essays on Rawls can be found in Norman Daniels, *Reading Rawls* (New York: Basic Books, 1977). A highly recommended but, unfortunately, very expensive general reference work is Peter Singer's *Companion to Ethics* (Oxford: Blackwell, 1991).

Index